Why French Women Wear Vintage

and other secrets of sustainable style

An Hachette UK Company
www.hachette.co.uk

First published in Great Britain in 2020 by Mitchell Beazley,
an imprint of Octopus Publishing Group Ltd
Carmelite House
50 Victoria Embankment
London EC4Y 0DZ
www.octopusbooks.co.uk

Distributed in the US by
Hachette Book Group
1290 Avenue of the Americas
4th and 5th Floors
New York, NY 10104

Distributed in Canada by
Canadian Manda Group
664 Annette St., Toronto,
Ontario, Canada M6S 2C8

ISBN 978-1-78472-669-0

A CIP catalogue record for this book is available from the British Library.

Printed and bound in China

10 9 8 7 6 5 4 3 2 1

Publisher: Alison Starling
Senior Editor: Pollyanna Poulter
Art Director: Juliette Norsworthy
Designer: Ben Brannan
Production Controller: Emily Noto
Copy Editor: Robert Anderson
Proofreader: Emily Preece-Morrison
Indexer: Isobel McLean
Photographer: Irma Notorahardjo
Illustrator: Jessica Durrant

Aloïs Guinut

Why French Women Wear Vintage

and other secrets
of sustainable style

Illustration Jessica Durrant
Photography Irma Notorahardjo

MITCHELL BEAZLEY

Contents

Introduction
6

Chapter 1
Wear Your Closet
12

Chapter 2
Heritage
54

Chapter 3
The New Rules
of Shopping
130

Chapter 4
Quality is Queen
160

Chapter 5
Max Out The Lifespan
192

Index
220

**References and
Contributors**
223

Acknowledgements
224

Introduction

Strolling through the commercial district of a foreign city, the world's traveller is struck by a feeling of déjà vu. The luxury boutiques and the clothing chains, down to the lettering, the smell and the music, all seem familiar. In search of a more exotic, authentic experience, she makes her escape from the crowds of tourists and darts into a narrow side street, only to find more of the same: Instagrammable shops approved by the trendy influencers with thousands of followers worldwide.

Over the last decade, entire neighbourhoods have lost their identity to the ever-growing clothing retail market. Since my first visit to the Marais quarter of Paris in 2003, I have seen the area shift from a charming, off-beat district featuring a mix of up-and-coming designers, traditional ateliers, bookstores and boulangeries to what amounts to an open-air shopping mall dominated by international brands. In the last five years, an antique shop has been replaced by a chic clothing store and the last neighbourhood supermarket transformed into a three-storey flagship of one of the clothing giants. The old quarter is now only faintly visible, like writing on a medieval palimpsest: overhanging the gleaming sign of a sleek clothes shop, on a faded ceramic fascia board, is written 'BOULANGERIE'.

In economically developed countries, people's motivations for spending money have long since shifted from needs to desires. There's no denying we need places to live in, food to nourish us and clothes to dress ourselves in, and, while we're at it, we might as well do these things with a certain degree of refinement to help make life as pleasurable as possible. But when did the clothing industry turn into little more than a cash machine whose main purpose seems to be its own never-ending growth?

Just as clothing retail shops are sucking the identity out of entire neighbourhoods, so that the architecture becomes little more than a backdrop for their products, the production of the garments they sell is eating away at the Earth's resources and the life of the workers who are producing them. Fashion has become the second most polluting industry in the world. And with what result? Our wardrobes are cluttered with so many clothes that the mere sight of them becomes overwhelming, yet at the same time we feel a constant craving for the next purchase that will transform our look.

It is time we reclaimed fashion back. To decide what we *want* to buy and not to be enticed into buying what we do not. We must acknowledge the environmental and ethical consequences of our purchases.

My Journey to Eco-conscious Style

I am passionate about all things beautiful and I cherish creativity in all its aspects. Wonderful architecture, tasteful interior decor, alluring fragrances, delicious food served on lovely plates, and vibrant music contribute to my everyday sense of wellbeing. Being surrounded by well-dressed people contributes to my daily aesthetic fix and keeps my happiness level up. Nothing upsets me more than a beautiful setting with poorly dressed people inside (OK, so I may be taking things a bit far here).

From an early age, dressing up was one of my favourite activities (aside from reading books, which led me to write books about

dressing up…*Oh, la vie!*). Now I'm an adult, combining colours, shapes and fabrics, and adapting my makeup, to create a renewed version of myself each morning still makes me happy. I also love searching for my 'ingredients' (the clothes) through a myriad of boutiques and online providers. The thrill of discovering a unique gem of an item that I can team up with my other belongings is truly blissful.

For much of the time, I did all this, let's say, thoughtlessly of the impact my behaviours had on the world around me. Then, in 2013, I decided to wean myself off fast fashion. Even though I had never been a big spender, I had a few relapses. But growing ecological concerns made me commit to my resolution for good. I can proudly claim that, at the time of writing in late 2019, I am now three years fast-fashion-free. However, the more I have looked into things, the more I have realized that the path to eco-conscious fashion is full of booby-traps:
• The eco-friendly market, though constantly evolving, is still niche and features few stylish products – not enough for a fashion-lover like me.
• Buying better-quality clothes is complicated, as finding out the manufacturing process, the country of origin of the materials, and the exact makeup of ALL clothes is super-difficult.
• Synthetic, oil-based fabrics are literally EVERYWHERE.

And then, I (re-)discovered vintage. Ah, I thought, could this be the solution to all my dilemmas? What could be more eco-friendly than something that has already been produced? I had been buying second-hand from my early student years and had always thought of it as a fun, alternative way to dress, so it was not exactly foreign to me. I once again took the plunge and began exploring the possibilities.

The bonuses of vintage shopping are:
• better quality for cheaper prices (as the overall quality of clothes has steadily declined over recent decades)
• unique pieces
• the fun of the search.

I am not going to lie, dressing sustainably in a stylish way is a challenge. When you buy in regular shops, you just have to copy and paste the looks from the mannequins. Buying less, buying better and thrifting requires more investment in terms of both time and creativity from you. But it's your way of taking back control of what enters your closet. In turn, our behavioural shifts will lead to shifts in the industry. And trust me, it feels rewarding and…it's fun! You'll enjoy exploring off-the-beaten-path shops, bijou thrift stores, getting to know (the often enthusiastic) salespeople and supporting local designers. After that, you might not be tempted to enter a loud, over-lit anonymous chain store again.

The French and Eco-friendly Fashion Style

For decades, the belief that French people (and especially women) are the most stylish on the planet has given rise to hundreds of publications, books and influencers of all kinds, from Jane Birkin to Jeanne Damas. In 2018, even if I have never entirely taken this line (the legendary French style is elegant, witty and easy to reproduce, but is far from being the last word in fashion), I joined this ever-growing crew of 'French fashion advisors' with my first book, *Dress Like a Parisian*. In that book, I explained that at the core of French style was the ability to pick the right clothes and combine them in a certain way rather than reshaping the whole content of your wardrobe each time a new trend shows up. The focal point was to show the reader how to use their existing clothes rather than encouraging them to buy more.

Among the many comments I received from my readers, the most heart-warming were those stating that my book had helped them create outfits using items from their existing wardrobe. One German reader wrote: 'You can actually put the book next to your closet

'French people are suspicious of unusual trends'

and immediately start to find new French-inspired combinations for your clothes that are full of flair.' This set me thinking, and one year after the publication of *Dress Like a Parisian* I felt the need to explore the idea of how French style and eco-friendly fashion might be natural partners.

But something bothered me. Are the French really an eco-conscious people? The French lifestyle, like every other Western lifestyle, could not be sustained in terms of the Earth's resources if it were to be adopted by people globally. We don't look like much of a role model either – we have the world's fourth-highest number of H&M stores and we typically wear only 30 per cent of the clothes in our wardrobes (though this is more than most of our European peers). Nevertheless, I feel that a large proportion of my compatriots have a reasonable approach to the consumption of fashion.

I did some anecdotal research. As a personal stylist, I of course spend a lot of my time in shops, and am surprised how often I see tourists buying the latest trendy thing (hybrid sock running shoes and open furry mules spring to mind). Intrigued, I asked the salespeople if French people, too, were drawn to such 'it' things. Much to my relief, they straightaway answered that these items had no success with the locals. French people, you see, are suspicious of the more ephemeral or unusual trends. Like good wine, they'll wait until something matures

before purchasing it. That said, they're not entirely immune to trends. If something that looks like a future basic comes into fashion, they'll take the plunge. The success of plaid or leopard patterns, high-waisted jeans and espadrilles is proof enough.

The French are also prone to adopting trends you can create with little or no financial investment. All white in winter is the in thing? Easy, let's just take all the white in the closet and wear it all together. Big Eighties earrings are making a comeback? Let's call *maman* to see if she's kept the ones she was wearing in that family picture. Scarves used as a hair knot? Easy one – I'll try that. Raw-edge jeans? Let's cut that old pair I have. Etcetera, etcetera.

Lots of French people take pride in NOT being influenced by trends. A few months ago I conducted a series of street interviews for a podcast asking random people about the latest trends. All the most stylish women I encountered insisted they had no idea

what the current trends were and that they simply dressed to please themselves, despite the fact that they clearly *were* following these trends. I believe their response was a mixture of snobbery and truth: they follow such trends because they genuinely love them, not just because they are trends.

In a nutshell, we French shy away from making purchases on the basis of the crazier trends but are also daring enough to have fun…with what we have in our closet. It's a magic recipe for remaining up to date without spending a lot. This means buying just a few but well-chosen, long-lasting clothes – a very eco-friendly behaviour.

Do the Numbers Stack Up?

Since 2007, according to the Institut français de la mode (French Fashion Institute), the value of the French clothing market has dropped by 15 per cent. In this same study, 51 per cent of a panel of French women claimed to have bought fewer clothes in 2018 than in 2017, thereby showing a desire to downsize their wardrobe. Among those consuming less, 40 per cent claimed that ecological and ethical concerns motivated their choices. For these eco-conscious consumers low prices are not the priority, and they demand transparency about the production chain and the quality of the products. As a result, the sales of fast-fashion outlets are falling.

'Buy less, dress better and, in between, choose wisely'

Meanwhile, the second-hand market is booming. Once again according to the Institut français de la mode, the proportion of French people who buy second-hand clothes went from 15 per cent in 2009 to 30 per cent in 2018. The total value of the French second-hand market is estimated at 1 billion euros a year and a tremendous growth seems in the offing. These behaviours are rooted in a worldwide global movement triggered by environmental concerns. The eco-conscious US brand Reformation has met with phenomenal success; British designers Stella McCartney and Vivienne Westwood are sustainable fashion's best spokespersons; Germany is developing artificial fibres that do not harm the environment; and Italy is creating nylon from recycled plastic bottles, which is then used by a Swedish company to create tights. The sustainable fashion revolution has begun, and we must all be part of it.

Aloïs

@aloisparisian | dresslikeaparisian.com

11

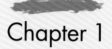

Chapter 1

Wear Your Closet

Prepare to Lay Your Closet Bare

Do you ever get that feeling, when standing in front of a closet full of clothes, of having nothing to wear? Often our solution is to go shopping. Yet did it ever occur to you that a new item might just end up making the problem worse? In other words: are our overstuffed wardrobes responsible for our lack of creativity?

In search of an answer, I paid a visit to my *grand-maman* Brigitte. I asked her whether, back in the 1970s when she was in her twenties, she wore all the clothes she owned. 'But of course!' she said with a shrug. My *mamie* was quite the fashionista at the time, loving to keep up with the latest fashions whether that was a long suede coat or knee-high boots. But she never made a purchase that she didn't go on to use. She only bought garments that she intended to wear – after all, she had saved hard for them. She NEVER bought for the thrill of the buy.

As a result of this policy, her closet was of a reasonable size. And yet she was considered to be a very stylish woman, someone who was creative by using different combinations of her limited resources, always wearing every single one of her precious possessions.

Fast-forward 50 years and most women's wardrobes have become gigantic clothes magnets, their contents a mystery to their owners. Overwhelmed by the endless choice, many of us end up wearing the same things over and over. We just reach for whatever is closest to hand.

To start your journey towards a leaner closet, I recommend that you undertake a massive decluttering exercise. This will result in you:
• owning fewer clothes
• knowing more about the items that you do own.

Imagine how you would feel, every morning, if you were faced with only pieces you were thrilled to wear and were already armed with plenty of creative ideas about how to combine them…

What a weight off your mind! What a joy!

'For more style,
let's start by having
fewer clothes'

My grand-maman in 1968 (pictured above)

Why We Accumulate Clothes

Brace yourself – it's time to discover what makes up that dreaded clutter in your closet. Take a deep breath, open your closet and take a look at your belongings. Roughly estimate what percentage you wear and what percentage you don't. The clothes you do not wear say something about your purchasing and hoarding patterns – and about *you*.

What's your clutter made up of?

Are they clothes you *used* to love?
- Happy memories are linked to them.
- They remind you of your youth.
- You used to feel so sexy in them.
=> *You are nostalgic.*

Are they clothes you *wish* you would wear...
- ...to those parties you *wish* you were invited to?
- ...for times when you feel more daring?
=> *You are a dreamer.*

Are they clothes that you think may *need* one day?
- Just in case you paint the spare bedroom/ mow the lawn/take part in a mud fight...?
=> *You are practical.*

Do you have *multiples* of the same thing (or variations on a theme)?
- Ten black T-shirts, everything with embroidery, Breton stripes galore...
=> *You are compulsive.*

Are they fashion *must-haves* from past seasons?
=> *You're a fashion addict.*

It's possible that you'll diagnose yourself as having multiple purchasing and hoarding patterns. Don't worry! We are about to embark on a decluttering process that will transform your habits.

Let the Decluttering Begin!

Gather all your clothes and accessories into one room. If this isn't possible, collect your shoes, coats and bags in another spot. Prepare to do some serious detective work: clothes may be hiding ANYWHERE in the house. Be meticulous and don't overlook a single cupboard or drawer. I've seen clients who have squirrelled away clothes in their attic, their cellar, a child's bedroom or even at their parents' house.

Don't exempt items. EVERYTHING is worth your consideration. Even *that* dinosaur-print T-shirt.

Relax – I'm not asking you to pile your belongings into a wrinkly mountain on your bed, *à la* Marie Kondo. My aim is to make you more stylish after all, not less. To achieve this, you need to be organized and certainly avoid any crinkling.

Sort your clothes and accessories into the following categories:
• everyday clothes
• occasion clothes
• shoes
• coats
• bags
• scarves, gloves, hats and glasses
• jewellery

Now divide each category into three piles:
• what you don't love anymore =>
The Unwanted
• what you *lurve* but never wear =>
The Crushes
• what you wear on a regular basis =>
The Dependables

The time has come to look at each pile and analyse its content. At this point, you may want to invite a friend over to help you decide what to keep. Often, we're not the best judges. A girlfriend with a flair for fashion is, of course, best. Ask her to be very – even ruthlessly – honest. Even better, hire a personal stylist (me! me! me!). A professional will help you make the *best* style choices.

What to Get Rid Of: The Unwanted

It seems that people aren't *that* bad a judge of their own clothes – 95 per cent of what is in the unwanted pile will end up being got rid of. In order to keep things efficient and not to exhaust you at the outset, I recommend that you don't try on most of the clothes in this pile.

There are a number of reasons why an item of clothing will have ended up in the 'unwanted' pile:

It's worn out

You had a fling with it and you've worn it quite a lot. Then suddenly the honeymoon was over and it seems like a shadow of its former self. But why did your relationship end so soon? Either the fabric was of poor quality, or the quality was excellent and you just loved it to death. (This can happen with lovers, too!)

Grieve for it a few moments. Accept that love is gone. Let it go in peace.

Lesson learned
If the item had a quick death, its quality was too low. If it has died after years of use and is beyond saving (*see* Chapter 5 for tips on maxing out the lifespan of your items), you are now doing the right thing by letting it go.

It's outdated

You can't quite put your finger on what's happened between you...Over the years, the appeal has faded and now you can't even bear to look at it. Be honest: how long since it last touched your skin? When did you buy it? If it was more than ten years ago, it's probably outdated. Be cautious: super-trendy items date much faster.

Most of this category will consist of fast-fashion impulse buys: say bye-bye *sans regret*. If they're designer items, your fashion-savvy friend or stylist may have a plan for them. If they still don't appeal, let them go.

Lesson learned
Think before you jump onto the latest trend.

It doesn't fit

You know, just by looking at it, that you're not a good match, but it is worth trying it on one last time to assess what's really wrong with it. Maybe the shirt collar is too high? Or the fabric of the trousers makes your thighs look thick? Or the pale green colour of the knitwear makes you look like a ghost?

Lesson learned
Know which shapes, fabrics and colours *don't* flatter you.

It's a 'plain Jane'

The item just makes you *yaaaawn*. There's nothing exciting about it. Perhaps it's a bad 'basic'? Be careful not to get rid of a useful, good-looking basic (*see* page 26). Otherwise, have no mercy.

Lesson learned
The basics are the most important pieces in your wardrobe. Choose stylish ones.

It's a mishap

There was always something not quite right about it. Take a closer look. Is that pocket in the wrong place? The hem uneven? The collar clunky? Does it make your butt look odd…?

Lesson learned
Pay attention to the detail and fit *before* buying.

What to Get Rid Of: The Crushes

You know those clothes you seem to keep hold of over the years even though they seem doomed to never see the light of day? Of course you do. Well, let's decipher what's wrong (or not!) with them. It's in this pile that I often find the forgotten treasures of my client's closets.

The nostalgic ones

'My old favourite jeans! The bag I bought with my first pay cheque! The shoes from when I worked in London!' Clothes carry memories. You could keep a few of these items for old times' sake.

The remedy
Check whether there's a way to update them.

Say goodbye if…
The items really are outdated/outworn or no longer match your personality/position.

The slim ones

This is another kind of nostalgia, for that time 'when I was thin'. The problem is that these items depress you on a daily basis.

The remedy
If the weight gain is temporary, be patient. If not, make peace with your new body shape and treat it to other, flattering styles.

Say goodbye if…
There is no way you'll get back to your previous figure.

The nowhere to wear

Dreaming of fancy dinners when in reality your meal partners are Netflix and a one-year-old practising his spoon skills? Own incredible dresses, low-cut tops and high heels, but never have a reason to wear them?

The remedy
• Buy glamorous stuff that you can wear in real life – let's say a pink jumper, printed boots with a reasonable heel height and a brown furry jacket.

• Try softening your fancy clothes with everyday casual garments. Team faux-diamond earrings with a loose jumper, a super-sexy top with jeans, a minidress with sneakers, and so on. Treat yourself by dressing fabulously *every* day.

Say goodbye if…
There is no chance you'll wear it again. If the sight of it in your closet depresses you…discard it.

The eccentrics

These are the flamboyant items that mesmerize you, but which you don't have the courage to actually pull out and pull on.

The remedy
How about taking baby steps? Tone down those loud items with your most basic pieces. Pair the crazy red biker jacket with black trousers, a grey T-shirt and black boots. Wear the heart-shaped glasses with a light, white summer dress.

Say goodbye if...
Even after trying the 'toning down' trick, you still feel like you're wearing a disguise. Take them out for a test drive, but if you spend the whole day desperate to change your outfit, take that as a sign.

The split personalities

The well-behaved girl you are can't keep her eyes away from her more cutting-edge peers. Once in a while, you wish you could just let loose with some punkish garments. Back at home with your avant-garde purchase, you look at those spiked shoes and wonder what on earth possessed you.

The remedy
Give your inner rebel a chance to express herself but wear the daring garment with your usual basics.

Say goodbye if...
You try the basics pairing and still feel like you are out in fancy dress.

The ones from a former life

When you got your first job, you pictured yourself as a modern-day Joan Holloway, parading about the office in tight dresses, fitted cardigans and high heels. As your career progressed, you grew more relaxed and replaced your dresses with trousers and your little cardigans with sweaters. Your closet is now brimming with clothes that no longer match your style.

The remedy
Change the way you wear the clothes. Pair them differently. Top your dress with a biker jacket, or tuck your cardigan inside high-waisted mom jeans.

Say goodbye if...
You really can't deal with how pink said cardigan is.

The worn-out ones (again)

You still love them, but when you put them on there's something not quite right. A fresh eye would tell you the truth. Things get old, *ma chérie*. Colours fade, threads pull, shapes distort...

The remedy
If the quality is top-notch AND you still love them, see whether there's a way to fix them (see page 205). If the quality is low, send them away to be recycled...and STOP buying fast fashion so the situation doesn't arise again

Say goodbye if...
There's no hope of a makeover.

What to Get Rid Of: The Dependables

A-ah! You weren't expecting the clothes you wear on a regular basis to be in the hot seat, were you? Just like your unwanted clothes, these too may be worn out, outdated or ill-fitting…but, because you are blinded by love, you don't see their flaws. To find out whether they're still worth keeping, get a fresh perspective. This can come from a trusted friend with a fashion flair, a professional stylist or…yourself. Consider each piece of clothing and ask:

• Is this worn out?
• If it is, can it be fixed?
• Does it flatter me? (The current 'me', not the former 'me' or the ideal 'me'.)

Sometimes, the 'dependable' pile will contain some of the following:

Worn-out things (again)

If an item's flaws are just too visible for *le bon style*, it may be that they can't be fixed.

What to do with it
If the item isn't a necessity in your daily life, then you and it should part ways. If it's a staple you don't have an alternative for, keep it until you find a suitable replacement.

The lesson
Buy only quality items and maintain them.

Things that could do with some improvement

An item is OK, but could be better – a shirt that's slightly too tight in the arms, a sweater that pulls around the chest.

What to do with it
Keep it until you find the perfect replacement.

The lesson
Acknowledge the little flaws your clothes may have so you don't repeat the same mistakes when buying similar items in the future.

'Because you are blinded by love, you don't see their flaws'

Impossible matches

These are pieces that aren't especially crazy-looking yet feature my pet style peeve: the superfluous detail. Let's take as an example a well-cut, white T-shirt with sparkly gold stitching around the collar. Sounds like a good idea, doesn't it? But the gold stitching makes it impossible to wear with a necklace, and every outfit suddenly looks 'cute' because of it.

What to do with it
These clothes are doomed. Make an exception, though, where the detail is a true style statement, like a scalloped collar.

The lesson
Stop buying such clothes!

How is getting rid of my clothes eco-friendly?

In a book promoting eco-consciousness, it may sound strange to recommend getting rid of lots of clothes, including some that you wear on a regular basis. However, I strongly believe decluttering your closet will lower your clothing consumption. Specifically:

• By assessing the contents of your wardrobe you will be able to stop making bad purchases.

• A wardrobe filled with things you love will enable you to create better outfit combinations and reduce your urge to shop.

• The clothes you get rid of can be adopted by others or recycled.

Why I <u>Don't</u> Believe in The 'Six-month No Wear, Get Rid of It' Rule

Many closet-editing gurus recommend getting rid of anything you haven't worn within the last six months. I vigorously disagree with this for the following reasons:

• If you live in a country with a temperate climate, chances are you use some of your wardrobe only half of the year.

• If you live in a tropical country, chances are you sometimes get out of your home country and experience some colder weather every few years.

• You may not have a super-fancy holiday every year, but when you do, that little dress you've been keeping hold of may well come in handy.

• You may not feel like wearing those green boots this year, but you still love them. Wait for their appeal to come back. Putting them on three years from now will feel like owning a brand-new pair.

• If a piece of unworn clothing falls into the 'love but do not wear' category, try finding a new use for it.

• Owning a few eccentric but cherished clothes that you only wear from time to time will prevent you from getting bored (and buying new clothes).

• Maybe that adorable scarf suits nothing in your wardrobe at the moment, but one day her Prince Charming may come and she'll be ready.

HOWEVER:

• Do not use my provisos as an excuse to store all your clothes just in case their flame revives. Only keep those items that you really do intend to wear again.

My trove of treasures that I may not wear everyday but love deeply

Keep the Basics

To guarantee you a perfect style without owning mountains of clothes and accessories, your wardrobe should contain only two categories of items: basics and statements. Each of your statement pieces should have at least one basic that can be worn alongside it, whereas your basics must be able to be combined together or spiced up with statements. *Et voilà.*

Pro tip

Embellishments with a bit of personality can transform your basic into a statement – such as a vintage, floral, embroidered shirt.

What's a basic?

A 'basic' is a 'fundamental' item. Consider your basics as the pillars of your wardrobe, the canvas for your painting… It should be neutral in colour and have a simple cut.

Asset
Versatility.

Risk
Boredom. A wardrobe made up solely of basics may leave you craving for another dimension to add to your outfits.

Keepers
- T-shirts: These can be used for layering.
- Shirts: Whether oversize, tight-fitting or something in-between, the versatility of the shirt is the greatest in the clothing kingdom.
- Knits and pullovers: The T-shirts of winter. If they're oversize, style them: tuck in the front, roll up the sleeves, add a belt or a necklace…
- Jean jackets, trench coats, tailored coats: Have I already said that layering is stylish?
- Simple, light items of jewellery: These could be in gold or silver and include white diamonds (real or fake).

What's NOT a basic?

Anything with an embellishment that makes it difficult to pair with something else – for example:
- A shirt with studs on the pockets
- A sweater with leather patches

Quality white shirt, impeccable black jeans, slick cowboy boots: an effortless look composed solely of basics

Lena Farouil

Fashion PR

Dress

I found it in Oslo in a beautiful thrift store six years ago when I was on a trip with my mum. *J'ai adoré* its Forties look. Mum got it for me, but when I came back I was not really ready to wear it (I was super-young). My friends said it was too 'grandma'. But for the last three years it's been a complete hit – everyone asks where I got it. It's in great condition; I just had to mend some stitches here and there. The brand name sounds totally Swedish – Ulf Andersson.

Watch

I found it just two days ago. I was in our country house where my mum keeps her vintage treasures. Each time I go, I scavenge for hidden gems. This time, I found a little box containing earrings and this bracelet watch, which is exactly my size. It makes me so happy because it's not easy to find bracelets for my thin wrists. My mother told me it came from my grandmother, who got it from her own mother!

Earrings

These were a gift from my paternal grandmother, who's from Guadeloupe. They used to be hers. She offered them to me when I had my ears pierced at ten years old. They're part of the traditional Guadeloupean outfit.

Glasses

I have had these for years. I adore their shape. I was really into that vintage style with the tortoiseshell. They are from Claire Goldsmith, the great-granddaughter of Oliver Goldsmith who created Audrey Hepburn's glasses in *Breakfast at Tiffany's*. I was so thrilled when the salesperson told me that, because she is my absolute style icon.

Espadrilles

I must confess they are a fast-fashion purchase from two summers ago in London…They are about to die now, but I liked their cute vintage vibe.

Keep the Statements

Now that we've covered the basics, let's add some spice…

What's a statement?

A garment that will make you look fabulous even if you pair it with the most basic of your basics.

Asset
Creativity.

Risks
Lack of versatility, eventually leading to boredom due to the same combination being worn on repeat.

Owning only statement items makes it impossible to create varied combinations.

Mixing several statement pieces together can work wonders but requires more developed styling skills.

Mild and strong statement items

Mild statement pieces
These are clothes and accessories that have only one outstanding thing about them. This might be an unusual colour, print or an interesting detail. They are versatile, combine well and will add loads of fun to your style.

Examples: A leopard-print shirt, red boots, a Prince of Wales blazer.

Strong statement pieces
These pieces qualify as 'really out there'. When you wear them, they 'swallow up' the whole look.

Examples: A star-printed oversize bomber jacket; metallic green pants.

Pro tips

• Keep only the strong statement pieces that you cherish and are likely to cherish for years. Wear them with matching basics when you're in the mood. It's OK to keep these, but only if you take them out for a spin once in a while!

• If your statement clothes have been gathering dust in your closet for too long, wear them for a day. Combine them with basics and see how you feel. If you spend every moment desperate to get out of it, then it's not for you or your wardrobe.

A black blazer frames Gisele's (see page 210) red silk statement dress perfectly

Nadia Chu

Artist

Shoes
When I moved to Paris from Vancouver five years ago, I loved Sandro, where I got these boots. My style quickly evolved, so I don't own much from them now, but these boots are a wardrobe staple.

Jeans
I found them at a hippy market. I was looking for black jeans, kind of 'boyfriend' type but not quite as large, and I found these red ones, too. Since red is my favourite colour, I took both!

T-shirt
This comes from Maison Standards. I instantly loved this brand because they sell amazing basics: they're well designed and manufactured using high-quality fabrics.

Jacket
It's vintage Thierry Mugler. It's actually part of a suit my friend Victoria bought for herself, as she's a big fan of the designer. She bought it online but it was too small for her. She instantly thought the suit would be perfect for me. So when I saw her a couple of weeks ago she gave it to me as a present.

Rings
I found them on a trip to Vancouver in a little boutique like Deyrolles [a centuries-old Parisian taxidermy and curiosity shop].

Choker
This is a handmade piece. I found a shop in the Marais that does leather pieces for people who are into BDSM. I noticed a man manufacturing leather inside, so I entered and asked if they could do bespoke. 'Of course!' he said. I chose the colours (red and black) and made it part of my look today as it was on the hanger with the jacket. I don't have a lot of space at home, so I often hang things I wear together on the same hanger.

'Black and red is my signature style'

Style

I feel at home in France. When I was in
Vancouver, my way of dressing wasn't
really appreciated. It's not a city of fashion.
What I notice in Paris is that you get an
education about fashion. Good fabrics,
perfectly cut timeless pieces…But I already
had all this inside me. My mother, who was
a seamstress, taught me what a good fabric
is. In Canada, I felt like a fish out of water.
In France, I found where I belong – not only
fashion-wise but culture-wise. My parents,
who came from Shanghai and Hong Kong,
really valued both good food and good
fashion, so every day I make an effort with
those two things.

Makeup and grooming

One of the first things that struck me when
I moved to Paris was the effortless grooming
style of the women. In Canada, they wear a
full face of makeup. I arrived in Paris with
very few makeup items in my luggage. Now,
I like to play with makeup. When I go out,
I can do something really spectacular, but
on an everyday basis I often only do lipstick.
Very easy and it takes less than two minutes.

*'I often hang
things I wear
together on the
same hanger'*

Get Rid of the (Evil) Twins

Now that you've got rid of the hopeless cases and identified your keepers, there might still be room for even more decluttering. I'm talking about what I call the 'evil twins'. To track them down, you'll have to start on another round of sorting:

1. Sort out your clothes according to type (trousers, skirts, jumpers).
2. Next, sort each type by colour. If you have a rack, create a rainbow; otherwise form piles on the floor.
3. If you have several items in the same category and colour, take note of the difference (or lack of) between them (for example, a deep-black sweater versus a light-black sweater).

You'll probably soon notice that you have favourite shades. You may even diagnose, dare I say it, an ADDICTION – perhaps to black bags, gold earrings or grey jackets. Usually, the endlessly repeated item is a basic: I have never encountered anyone with a collecting fetish for pink shoes, while I have witnessed many an obsession with pairs of black boots.

Think about *your* addiction, if you have one: each time you spot a variation of it in a shop, is it love at first sight? Do you just *have* to buy it? Do you think: 'What if there's a shortage of long-sleeved, navy-blue tops in the future? And this one is excellent! And I wear a lot of things like this, so it's a really useful purchase'? Well, the straight answer is: NO, IT'S NOT. There are only seven days in a week, and, unless you're aiming for a Mark Zuckerberg way of life, you most likely won't wear navy-blue, long-sleeved tops more than three days a week.

Sorting your clothes as twins will help you determine:
• what you buy too much of
• what you need to stop buying.

Recognize That Life Changes and Clothes Change With It

Sometimes, while our clothes are still perfectly wearable, they simply aren't for us anymore. Realizing and understanding that we have changed physically and/or mentally can be a difficult process.

Weight fluctuations

If you're prone to weight fluctuations, you'll know that jeans are the most unforgiving piece of your wardrobe because, unlike dresses or skirts, they're unable to adapt. Which can be a pickle because they have become the ultimate staple of our Western wardrobes. When I start the process of closet editing, I ask my clients to show me their most flattering jeans and then the ones they *don't* wear. 'What's wrong with them?' I ask. 'Well, if I dropped/gained a few kilos,' they reply, 'I would gladly wear them again.'

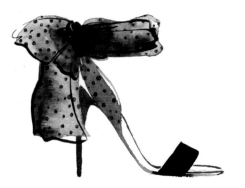

To determine whether you should keep such items, ask yourself honestly if your current weight is here to stay. Ask yourself:
• Was your former weight achieved through intensive dieting? Or after a bad breakup? *That was probably not your normal weight. You can safely get rid of the clothes.*
• Is your current weight unusual for you? Have you recently been pregnant or too busy moving house to eat well? *Keep the clothes for now – you'll probably get back to your former weight.*

Lifestyle changes

The main function of our clothes is to allow us to dress both for the climate and for our job. If you move to another country – say, from rainy UK to sunny Italy – your wardrobe will necessarily undergo a transformation. The day you decide to leave your job as a biologist to become a stand-up comedian, chances are your wardrobe will take a new direction.

To determine if you should keep an item of clothing, ask yourself whether you might need it again in the future:
• Do you plan to stay in your new country for more than five years?
• Is there a possibility of going back to your old job, if your new career doesn't take off?

How to Cure Unwanted Behavioural Patterns

Congratulations, now that you're more familiar with your wardrobe clutter, you should be able to determine which of the style personality types (*see* page 16) you belong to and how to address your behaviour. Here are some easy cures:

You're nostalgic

• Donate your clothes so that others can have great experiences wearing them.
• Revamp some of your beloved garments to create new styles.
• Create a small box of 'treasured items' for the future you or for those who come after you.

You're a dreamer

• Stop buying clothes you won't wear.
• Accept your body shape and buy clothes that flatter the REAL you.
• Know your own personality and buy accordingly.
• Tone down the style of over-dressy items you own by wearing them with casual basics.
• Get rid of shoes you can't walk in and dresses you can't breathe in.

You're practical

• Determine how many of each practical item you really need.
• Stop 'double-buying' things because they fit and are comfy.

You're compulsive

• Acknowledge your obsessions, stop pandering to them and work with what you have.
• If you buy the same over and over, decide which is your favourite and stick to wearing it. The others are just 'evil twins' (see page 35).

You're a fashion addict

• Before you buy anything, ask yourself whether you love it or just want to be trendy.

A Lesson in Style-proofing

You should now have only *la crème de la crème* in your wardrobe – the perfect ingredients to start styling with. For greater efficiency and effectiveness, you could have this task done by a personal stylist or get help from a stylish friend. Either way, by the end of this lesson there should be no item of clothing in your closet that doesn't belong to an outfit.

1. Choose a basic foundation and start pairing

For instance, put on a pair of jeans, add a white T-shirt and see how many layering and accessorizing options you can pair with that base.

2. Get creative over the basic foundation

- Change the shoes – sandals, loafers, heels…– and roll up the jeans accordingly.
- Try adding accessories – belts, scarves, hats…
- Tuck or untuck the top.
- Try layering: dressy jackets, casual jackets, oversize shirts worn open over T-shirts…
- Add jewellery: classy strings of pearls, layered necklaces, multiple rings, statement earrings…

3. Replace the basic top with another and repeat the process

Try replacing the T-shirt with a shirt or a sweater and repeat. The difference in shape will create different options.

4. Once you've tried all your basic tops, move on to your statement tops

Start with more 'neutral' accessorizing. If you feel inspired, try out more daring or unusual combinations.

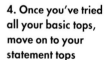

Pro tip

Don't be afraid of trying crazy combinations!

5. Repeat with bottom items and dresses

Tackle all your basic bottom options first, then move on to your statement ones. Repeat the process with your dresses.

6. Try to combine the statement pieces you haven't used yet

If you get stuck over a statement piece, try wearing it with one of your most basic items. If you still aren't satisfied:
• ask for help from a skilled friend or stylist
• purchase the basic you need to go with it.

A simple adjustment can give a basic item a whole new style

The Perfect Wardrobe Foundation – A Checklist

During the style-proofing process on page 38, you may have encountered a few difficulties when trying to put together outfits. Ninety-nine per cent of the time, this is down to a shortage of good basics. Here is my list of basics that will enable you to combine ANY items together. All the clothes in the list below should be in a neutral colour: black, navy blue, grey or beige. All of them should be alluring in their simplicity, and the fabric and cut should be of the very best.

• 1 sweater in a smooth fabric and light colour
• 1 sweater in a smooth fabric and dark colour
• 3 white T-shirts (can include a crew neck and a scoop neck as well as different fabrics)
• 1 T-shirt in a dark colour (grey or black)
• 1 white shirt
• 1 blazer (black, navy or grey)
• 1 mid-season coat (jean jacket, trench coat, lightweight coat – whatever suits your lifestyle)
• 1 warm coat
• 3 pairs of jeans (a combination of different colours and shapes)
• 3 elegant pairs of trousers or skirts (if you work in a formal environment)
• 1 pair of walkable sandals for summer (flats or low platforms)

• 1 pair of walkable closed shoes for winter (flats or boots)
• 1 pair of fancy shoes for special occasions
• 1 scarf
• 1 beanie (or other hat)
• 1 belt for jeans
• 1 simple necklace or pair of earrings
• 1 ring/bracelet combination for everyday wear
• 1 day bag big enough to carry everything
• 1 fancy bag for evenings out

This adds up to a total wardrobe base of 26 items.

To this you can add 'the spice' – some of those mild and strong statement clothes we looked at on page 30.

Pro tips

- Because dresses are usually self-sufficient, I don't include them in outfit combinations.
- Make this list your own. This one is designed for people living in a temperate climate, so you may need to make adjustments if you live somewhere that is very cold or very hot all year round. And if you're not a jeans or blazer person…just skip those items.

Where to Donate

As you sit next to your pile of discarded clothes, you may be wondering what on earth you are going to do with them. You're probably sensitive to the fact that just leaving them in the garbage is not a very eco-conscious behaviour. Here are my suggestions:

Worn-out items

These are simply too damaged to be worn by anyone.

Take them to the charity shop
While the charity won't be able to sell them, they will be able to recycle their fibres.

Pro tip

If you have a substantial amount of branded clothing, some consignment stores will pay a visit to your home and review your closet.

Worthless items

These are fast-fashion clothes that are OK but have no retail worth.

Take them to the charity shop
An easy solution that will help raise funds for a good cause.

Online second-hand stores
I would avoid selling online by yourself, which is super-time-consuming for very little money.

Consignment stores
Be aware that boutique consignment stores usually do not accept fast fashion.

Branded items

These are items from fashionable, quality brands that are in good condition.

Drop them at a charity shop
Because why not? You'll be donating to a worthwhile cause and will swiftly be rid of your clothes. Quality donations of this kind provide charities with a healthy income.

Sell them online
Try listing them on specialized websites. Pamper your pieces, take good pictures, add a price, write a description (mentioning any flaws), and wait for someone to get hooked.

Take them to a consignment store
These stores are very picky. Your clothes must be fashionable (or have come back into fashion) and in perfect condition. If the condition isn't excellent but the brand is super-prestigious, the store may do any repairs for you. These stores offer you a good way to make money without having the hassle of displaying the clothes online yourself.

A good resolution for the weekend: drop the clothes you do not use at the charity shop

Upscale Your Storage to Improve Your Style

One of the main reasons we wear such a disappointingly low percentage of our clothes is because we simply don't see them. As the traditional French saying goes: *loin des yeux, loin du cœur* (literally, 'far from the eyes, far from the heart'). If you make sure all your clothes and accessories are visible and easy to reach, then you'll wear them.

The benefits of seasonal storage

So that we can keep our clothes in plain sight, let's paradoxically begin by hiding (some of) them. Some wardrobe gurus advise us to keep EVERYTHING in the closet, regardless of the season. I disagree for the following reasons:

1 Lack of room

Most of us, especially the *Parisiennes*, Londoners, New Yorkers, Hongkongers and Tokyoites among us (i.e. those who live in places where a square metre costs twice as much as a Chanel bag), simply do not have enough room in our wardrobes, even after an efficient decluttering. Besides, nicely spaced-out hangers provide a much more pleasant view, don't they?

2 The joy of reunions

Storing the clothes you won't use for a few months is like saying goodbye to a dear friend who lives far away. When they come back, you'll be thrilled to see them again. 'Aw, pink sandals, I missed you so, so much this cold winter.'

3 A twice-yearly check-up

Each time you put your seasonal clothes aside, you're obliged to take a good look at them. The same happens when you take them out again. Twice a year, your memory will be jogged about what you own and you'll have the chance to get rid of anything you're tired of.

4 A clearer closet

The whole aim of clearing up the closet is not having to deal with the daily sight of garments you won't wear. In the same spirit, spare yourself the sight of dainty sandals and flimsy linen dresses when a Siberian wind is raging outside.

Shoes

Where?

- Ideally, next to the front door (seasonal shoes only; store other shoes elsewhere).

How?

- On shoe racks or shelves where they're all visible.
- Arranged according to height and type/use.
- On each shelf, create a 'rainbow' from light to dark.
- I recommend that you display your shoes 'naked', so that you can see them.
- Some people prefer to store their shoes cossetted inside their boxes. If you do this, stick a photograph of the shoes on the box.

Like a boss

You could invest in a custom-made shoe rack or shelf, taking into account:
- the size of your apartment/house
- the height of your shoes
- whether you'll want to close a door on them so you hide the mess.

Suggested categories

- Fancy high heels.
- Comfortable daytime heels.
- Flats.
- Sneakers (if you require a second line of flats).

Pro tips

- You can use seasonal storage for your shoes, but keep one pair of heeled sandals to wear with tights in the autumn.
- Using shoe trees will improve the lifespan of your shoes.

Hanging clothes

Where?

- In your closet.
- In your dedicated dressing room (I envy you, Carrie B).
- Displayed on a curated rack (I admire your minimalist approach).

What?

- *Mandatory:* Anything that wrinkles and/or cannot be folded – for example, coats, jackets, shirts, blouses, dresses, trousers.
- *Forbidden:* Knitwear. Hangers will make them lose their shape.
- *Optional:* If you have the space, hang your jeans so that you can see them better.

How?

Get a set of matching hangers
They will make your closet look so much more organized. These should include:
- basic wooden ones for all ordinary clothes
- large shoulder ones for heavy jackets
- padded ones for delicates (silk, lace and other fragile items)
- trouser hangers
- padded clip hangers for skirts.

Sort your clothes according to category
In each category, sort items according to colour (create a rainbow). If need be, create a special 'long-length' mixed category. This will help you find your clothes quickly when you're getting ready for work.

Pro tips

Hanging clothes
- Keep a few summer dresses in your winter wardrobe. You'll be able to style them with tights, boots and sweaters.
- What about those super-thin wire hangers that seem to multiply more quickly than rabbits? They're mean to your clothes, so keeping them is not an option. The most eco-conscious solution is to close the loop and give them back to your dry cleaner.

Folded clothes
(*see opposite*)
- If you don't have a chest of drawers, buy boxes for your closet and use them instead.

Folded clothes

Where?

- On shelves.
- In drawers.

What?

- T-shirts, knits, sweaters – anything that would be put out of shape on a hanger.
- Jeans do well folded.

How?

There are two methods:

KonMari (best)
To be honest, I wish I had discovered Marie Kondo, the Japanese high priestess of tidying, before I purchased my closet. Her 'vertical fold' method is the best way to store your clothes, so that you can see every shape and design as soon as you open your drawer, while maximizing use of space.

Classic
Fold and stack your T-shirts and knits on top of one another. Put the fragile ones into a different pile from the thicker ones. Avoid crushing delicate knits under a pile of heavier ones, as this could damage the fibres. If required/possible, install more shelves in your closet to reduce the size of the piles.

Sort your folded clothes in the following way:
- *In a drawer:* Create a rainbow.
- *On shelves:* Create a stack of neutral and a stack of coloured and printed.

Jewellery

Where?

- In your room.
- In your closet.
- In a dedicated dresser.

Why?

Your goals here are to:
- see everything
- dodge tangles and knots.

What and how?

Necklaces

- Hang on little hooks either inside your closet or in your room as a decorative element.
- The statement ones that cannot be hung up can be placed in stackable trays.
- Aim to have a tray per necklace. You can stack the trays one on top of the other.
- Smaller necklaces that aren't at risk of becoming tangled can be placed in a compartmentalized tray.

Bracelets

- Place in a dedicated compartmentalized tray.
- Alternatively, display on a circular rack as in a shop.

Rings

- Use a dedicated compartmentalized tray for long-term storage of rings.
- If you have few rings, or a cherished set of rings that you wear every day, place a little dish by your washbasin so you can store them safely when you wash your hands.

Earrings

- Opt for a compartmentalized tray with small cells for studs and big cells for pendants or hoops.
- You can use the little ring dish (mentioned above) to store your earrings when cleansing your face.

Pro tip

Instead of stackable trays, try a jewellery box, or a specially designed dresser that suits your storage needs. If you use/change your jewellery on a regular basis, drawers will be easier to handle than a pile of trays.

Scarves

Where?

- In your closet.
- Next to your coats.
- Next to the front door.

How?

- Rolled up and stored in a compartmentalized unit is the least space-consuming option.
- Hung next to your jackets, or laid flat inside a drawer or in a box.
- Alternatively, hang them on hooks: this only works if you have just a few scarves or lots of room. You could use a dedicated scarf hanger or pegs in your entrance hall. Beware, such a hanger will quickly look messy, especially if it's the first thing you see on entering the house.
- Store heavy- and lightweight scarves in different places.

Gloves

Where?

- Next to your coats.
- Next to the front door.

How?

- A box or a dedicated drawer is optimal.

Socks and tights

Where?

- In your closet, inside a dedicated drawer or box.

How?

- If you have space, I have nothing against the classic 'balled-up' way of storing socks.
- By contrast, however, I prefer to lay tights flat, creating a rainbow.
- The perfectionist can Marie Kondo her drawers by folding her socks and tights and displaying them in compartmentalized boxes/drawers.

Glasses

Where?

- In your closet.
- Somewhere in your bedroom/dressing room.

How?

- If you have just a few pairs, keep each in its case, somewhere easily accessible. You won't need to see them as you'll know which case they are in.
- If you have more than five pairs, place them in a dedicated display case or drawer, as in a shop counter display. Ideally, the bottom of the display case should be soft to prevent scratches.

Belts

Where?

- In your closet.

How?

- Roll them up and put them into a drawer. If you don't have a drawer, get a compartmentalized box for a neater result.
- If you prefer, hang them on a dedicated hanger or on hooks.

Pro tip

Internet-search each of these categories for extra visual inspiration and to find the unique storage solution that appeals to you.

Bags

Where?

- Keep the bags that you use a lot in/near the entrance hall.
- Store any fancy or occasion bags in your closet.

How?

It all depends on the number of bags you own and their nature:

- Place the ones you use every week near your front door, on a shelf, in a standing position.
- Store clutch bags in a dedicated box or drawer, in a standing position.
- If you have a lot of other bags, try to place them on shelves, next to one another, and in a standing position. This is the best way not to damage them. You can use shelf dividers. The bags could have a decorative function in the room.

Makeup

I consider makeup an accessory. Bright lips, statement liner or varnished nails have the capacity to completely change a look. Just as with messily stored clothes, keeping too much makeup in a chaotic fashion leads you to buy unnecessary new items. Here, impulse buys can be even more tempting given the small size and relatively low prices of these items. This leads to many women owning several bags of makeup that they never use. It's time to give your makeup collection a make-under.

Pro tip

Swear to finish every last drop of a classic product before you buy a new one. There's no need to own countless identical mascaras, eyeliners and bronzers.

Step 1: Sorting

- Gather together your daily essentials, so they are safe.
- Smell- and texture-proof all the remaining items. Odd scent? Bye-bye. Sticky? *Adios*.
- Try on any colour you're not sure about. Does that red lipstick wonderfully bring out your teeth's yellow undertones? *Tchüss*.
- Classify your makeup by category. The more products you own, the more precise the categories can be.

Step 2: Organizing

- Display your essentials next to your mirror. Use a jar for your pencils, mascaras and brushes. The remaining items can be put on a shelf or in a case.
- Put what you use less often in a specially designed vanity with compartments or compartmentalized drawers.

Step 3: Get creative... or don't

- If you don't want to take the time to come up with different ways of applying your makeup, stick to your essentials and create yourself a super-minimal makeup counter.
- If you want to be more creative, try using the unusual things in your collection. Get inspired! Green eyeliner/bright coral lips/glittery eyelids... Dare to wear as a solo statement, eventually adding foundation, then a hint of blusher and mascara.

Chapter 2

Heritage

Fashion is About Heritage

As far as I remember, I have always played with clothes. Most likely, it's something in my genes. I grew up in La Rochelle on the Atlantic coast, the eldest of five sisters. My mother, a fashion lover herself, would always pick the most adorable things for us. Well, for me mostly: one of the perks of being the firstborn is getting brand-new stuff. From an early age, I asked my mother to let me accompany her to the boutiques. These shopping trips provided me with precious one-to-one moments with my working *maman*. She was the perfect shopping partner, providing both excellent style advice and funds. I enjoyed those shared times that went beyond just clothes.

Over my teenage years, I reproduced those moments of styling intimacy with my best friend, who, being a little less fashion-savvy than me, had asked me to be her shopping partner. I was flattered and genuinely happy to help her feel confident with her look. Don't get me wrong, I was no high-school princess; more the discreet witty nerd who used fashion as a way to empower herself.

At home, I staged 'fashion shows' using my little sisters as models and my mother's, grandmother's and even my father's old garments as the base for my creations. I would imagine a background story for every costume and take care of every detail, from the makeup to the setting of the occasional photoshoot. Last year, one of my sisters dug up an old video of one of those homemade catwalk shows. My younger sisters are all dressed up and parading about in their outfits in front of my parents. In the background, an 11-year-old me is directing the whole affair. At the end, you can hear my father asking who the *modiste* was. I promptly correct him: 'La *styliste*! C'est moi.'

Later, as a teenager, I opened the dressing-up box again. Some of the clothes were now my size. Embroidered cottons, long hippie skirts, tight leather. I adopted them into my wardrobe. Some are still there. Even as an adult, I still regularly ask my mother to donate me clothes for which she no longer has any use. They all have *ce petit supplément d'âme* (that little extra bit of soul) that other clothes do not.

Immaterial heritage

This is the intangible heritage – or cultural legacy – you have from your family, friends and surroundings…and, of course, the country you live in – ideas, values, that certain something called style. It may be the case that you build your style in opposition to this heritage.

Material heritage

This is made up of the actual things that you 'inherit' from family and friends…or even from yourself! An example of the last could be the bag you bought with your first salary or the dress you wore to your best friend's wedding. More generally, it could be the heritage of decades of French fashion, accumulated in closets through the magic of thrift shops.

'This is the best form of recycling'

A Chanel-inspired jacket worn with modern basics: timeless and versatile

Grandmère Coco's Legacy

In the 1928 picture illustrating her Wikipedia page, Gabrielle ('Coco') Chanel is wearing a *marinière* (Breton top) tucked into wide-leg trousers, her waist highlighted by a black belt, hands in pockets in a relaxed pose. Minus the hair – too stiff for today's taste – the photograph could have been taken yesterday.

Through the lens of eco-consciousness, what's more sustainable than a 'timeless look'? I have looked at dozens of pictures of iconic French actresses and celebrities throughout the twentieth century and their outfits look so contemporary I would happily wear any of them. Often their haircut, makeup, jewellery, skirt length or shoulder shape will betray the decade in which the picture was shot. Yet sometimes you have to look at details as subtle as the film grain or the pose to date an image.

Coco Chanel made simplicity the essence of Parisian style, and it has been an unwritten rule ever since. The simplicity and comfort she brought into fashion were a true revolution back in 1920. This schism put an end to centuries of imprisonment of the female body. Clothing went from being decorative and restrictive to being liberating and designed for the independent woman. Gabrielle Chanel herself was the embodiment of freedom, running her own business as a single woman.

As the decades have passed, trends have changed at a steadily increasing rate. The 1920s freed women's bodies; the Thirties defined a new femininity; the Forties and Fifties saw the rise of modern glamour; the Sixties instigated a youthful style; the Seventies took on board both hippie and bourgeois vibes; the Eighties empowered women so they could enjoy both feminine and masculine dress codes; the Nineties made street-style fashionable while glorifying minimalism, while the Noughties were all about bling, fun and fame or rock, fun and fame (choose your team).

Today's French designers may seem to live on a different planet from Coco Chanel, but still her simplicity and comfort resonate.

French style combines the simple and the over-the-top in one wardrobe. 'Get the basics and season them to the season' might be the French style motto. Coco famously said, '*la mode se démode, le style reste*' (fashion goes out of fashion, style remains) – and Yves Saint Laurent, *grand-père* of French fashion, said pretty much the same.

Embrace the Eco-friendly Trend for Nostalgia

A hundred years of *prêt-à-porter* has generated enough nostalgia to inspire generations of stylists. Recently, the revival phenomenon seems to have increased. Has fashion nothing left to say, or does this peak fascination with former styles say something about our current aspirations? In an era where fashion has been found guilty of being the second most polluting industry in the world, can we still afford to produce sumptuous, luxurious attire whose appeal will be outdated by the following season? This may have been the hidden message behind Hedi Slimane's dejà-vu outfits for the Spring/Summer 2020 Céline catwalk show. There was nothing new, only a masterly reinterpretation of Céline Vipiana's Seventies silhouettes. Is looking back to the past the destiny of a fashion industry stuck in a 'no future' mood?

There's some good news here: we have a century of ready-to-wear at our disposal to create unique, modern looks. And there's more good news: we can turn our preoccupation with past styles to the advantage of our planet and the environment.

The internet and fashion

The internet has become part of our daily routine, delivering an unstoppable supply of information of all kinds. The fashion savvy use it to improve their knowledge, keeping up with that week's trends, scrolling through Instagram, Pinterest and YouTube in search of new inspiration and role models. Where designers and magazines used to set the tone, thousands of influencers, divided into tribes, now offer their own vision of fashion, be it vintage or contemporary.

If you aim to become a more eco-conscious buyer, start following influencers who share your beliefs. In France, eco-conscious bloggers, YouTubers and Instagrammers have been booming in the last few years. You can join the 100,000 followers of Clara Victorya, a twenty-something couture hacker who transforms rags into cool clothes. Vintage lovers will be inspired by Nawal Bonnefoy's quirky take on pinup style (*see* page 118) as well as by her confessions about her life as a former fast-fashion addict. Check out, too, Francine's chic and hip outfits (*see* pages 71 and 180).

Mathilde (see page 74) sporting a seventies-inspired outfit

What Does Heritage Mean to the French?

Your relatives are far from being your only provider of fashion culture:

• **Heritage from your friends and colleagues** In addition to the internet, your friends and colleagues can be your fashion educators. Hanging out with well-dressed people will train your eye without you even noticing it.

• **Heritage from your town/city** Where you live influences your style and level of elegance – whether out and about, at work or at a party. It tells you, for example, whether logos are tacky or chic, whether going out without makeup is acceptable or not. Whether you follow those rules or not, they become ingrained.

• **Heritage from your country** International press titles have totally different editions depending on the country they are published in. Just look at the covers of *Elle* from around the world. Similarly, the clothes displayed in the windows of international chains differ from one country to another. Independent shops accentuate this individuality still further. Accelerating globalization has not yet erased countries' unique fashion heritages.

Heritage over innovation

Heritage is a key value to consider when deciphering French style. The French are often made fun of because of their supposed arrogance and attachment to tradition. It's a cliché but it has some truth. Centuries of talented architects have created a gorgeous heritage in terms of the built environment. Food, too, is a national pride (it's considered blasphemous to criticize *la cuisine traditionelle*). Our language even has its own academy whose job is to protect and preserve it. Fashion is just one more part of a cultural heritage that the French can be super-smug about.

The bourgeois way

In 2004, the French brand Comptoir des Cotonniers became popular among teenagers thanks to their mother–daughter campaign featuring real families. The idea was that a young woman could be rebellious while still showing her love for *maman* through a shared passion for style. More than a decade later, the brand invited the girls featured in the 2004 adverts to a reunion. In a mini story video, Philippine, a chic blonde in her early thirties, tells the camera how she has been wearing the same pair of Comptoir shorts since she was 15, shows off a Comptoir trench coat she cherishes because it used to be her mother's ('It still smells like her'), and confesses to having stolen the same

Heritage also speaks to women of different ethnic backgrounds, who mix their parents' fashion heritage with that of their birth country. My friend Lan Anh, whose Vietnamese parents arrived in France in their early twenties, has noticed how she shares with the women in her family an attraction to bright colours and wonders whether this is related to traditional Vietnamese outfits. Her seamstress aunt often gives her old clothes, and these quickly blend into her wardrobe. Nevertheless, such trends tend to be 'smoothed over' in the face of the dominant French fashion culture. The heritage of the immigrant culture lies in the details.

Age increases value

As in many European countries with a long history, France cherishes *les vieilles choses* (old things) that are passed from one person to another, from one generation to the next. It may be a watch, a piece of jewellery, a scarf… As with a good wine, age increases its value. The emotional weight it carries increases, too.

brand's tops from her elder sister, before entering the kitchen to introduce us to her *madeleines de Proust* – a food that brings back childhood memories – and her grandfather's time-honoured *tarte aux pommes. Oh là là,* so many clichés about Frenchness and heritage in just one video…But can everyone relate to this?

Manon Ledet

Brand content manager

Bag

It's the Proenza Schouler 'PS11' that I have been coveting for the last ten years. I don't exactly remember how it became part of my wish list, but I do remember checking it out in real life at Printemps in Lille – the price really was too much for me. A few months ago, my desire for this bag resurfaced. In the meantime, I had become a pro in spotting stuff on second-hand apps. I found it on Vinted after six months of search alerts. The seller wanted to get rid of it quickly as it was a gift from her ex-boyfriend, so I was able to negotiate quite easily. It's exactly what I like in terms of shape and size. What caught my attention is the silver hardware that matches my jewellery.

I buy only the trends that are my style: classic with hints of rock attitude. As quality is super-important for me, I always check for the famous, well-established brands on second-hand apps – both for reasons of ecology and economy. If I don't find what I want, then I buy it new.

Trench

My friend is a freelance nurse. When he visits people, he always has a glance over what's been left outside as garbage to see whether there's anything clean to be had. One time, as he was leaving a chic, elderly lady, he spotted a bagful of clothes. There were two Hermès scarves and this Burberry trench! He asked her if he could take them, and he brought them back to me.

Trousers

They're an H&M pair I got on Vinted. I was looking for a large pair in a rust shade and ended up with these khaki ones, which do the job. They look as good with flat sneakers as they do with heels.

Shoes

These are brown croco-printed boots from Topshop. I had wanted them for more than six months when my grandma gave them to me as a Christmas gift. It was a thought-through choice, because they combine with almost anything in my wardrobe. That's the power of accessories and layers: you add them to a basic outfit to make it look as though you are wearing something completely different…when in reality you've only changed one thing.

Know Your Fashion History

Just as a good cook should have a command of the basics of cooking, and a talented interior designer should be well versed in the decorative arts, a stylish person should know about style history. The art of dressing well has a lot to do with your knowledge. The more you know about fashion the easier it will be for you to compose an outfit, whether while out shopping or from the 'ingredients' in your wardrobe. As French clothes guru Marc Beaugé has said: 'The more educated you get about fashion, the less you buy.'

I recommend that you start your fashion education in 1920, when women's bodies were being liberated from corsets and cumbersome dresses, thanks, among others, to *Grandmère* Coco (*see* page 59).

1. Inform yourself

- Purchase an illustrated book about the history of fashion through the 20th century and put it next to your bed (or in the loo, if you like – I'm not here to judge).

- Google your way through each decade to find the features you could replicate. For example, if you search 'Eighties fashion' you'll find articles from newspapers and blogs about the best of the decade's fashion. These pictures might inspire you to bring heavy costume jewellery, statement belts and shoulder pads into your life.

- Find historical style icons and Pinterest their style.

- Flip through the pages of old magazines.

2. Recognize the comebacks

Being more educated about fashion will help you notice revival trends (referred to on page 60). You will start recognizing them in the shops, in the media and on the catwalk. As I write this book, my fellow *Parisiennes* are busy reliving trends from the Eighties to the Noughties, though this may quickly change. Fashion is never far from pop culture. A few years ago, after the success of the movie *The Great Gatsby* (2013), there was a craze for Art Deco jewellery and dresses. *Mad Men* (2007–15) brought about a revival in the voluptuous pinup style of the Fifties. The current enthusiasm for the Eighties follows the success of Netflix shows such as *Stranger Things* (2016–) or *GLOW* (2017–20).

3. Apply your knowledge

What can you do with what you have? It's often just about the way you put clothes together. A knee-length dress with knee-high boots? Boom! – Seventies chic.

Start with accessories: ask your mother/grandmother whether she has anything from the Eighties, for instance. Look in your own wardrobe if you are old enough. Search in vintage shops…

Pick what you like best from the decade you fancy and mix it with the basic clothing you already own.

Nawal (see page 118) punctuates a nineties-style suit with seventies-inspired colouring

...But Also Know Current Trends

Even if the luxury industry (apart from a few designers) hasn't yet taken an eco-conscious path, looking at the shows is a useful experience for someone aiming to be sustainably stylish. Watching the new-season collections will inspire you to create new ways of combining what you already own with future vintage/second-hand/carefully chosen purchases.

The fast-fashion brands digest the shows' content as quickly as possible in order to produce low-quality duplicates. How about getting your inspiration from the source and digesting the material yourself? Go online and watch the shows (you'll find links on fashion magazine websites).

Pro tips

• Catwalks can be intimidating as they present very fashion-forward outfits, even if they also look back to the styles of the past. Your goal is to deconstruct what they're about in order to work out what you could realistically replicate in your daily life.

• If you are in love with a luxury piece, why not invest once in a while? It will last you a long time and may become the vintage of tomorrow.

What to look for on the catwalk

1. Choose the brands you like.

2. Pay attention to combinations of colours, prints and fabrics and try to replicate them.

3. Take note of the style features you could use, for example:
• wearing a bouffant shirt under a tight sleeveless sweater (Vuitton)
• replacing the plain buttons of your black blazer with ornamental ones (Miu Miu)
• wearing your cardigan low on the shoulders Bardot-style (Miu Miu)
• putting silky socks in your Mary Janes (APC)
• belting dresses with a gold chain (Céline).

Find Your Fashion-conscious Clique

Take a look at well-dressed people – in real life or on the Internet – and use their know-how to improve your fashion knowledge.

Follow eco-conscious style influencers

Whether on Instagram or on YouTube, find a virtual clique that shares your beliefs. Unsubscribe from any fast-fashion hauler or luxury addict girls. Instead, follow the clever thrifters, vintage divas or DIY queens. Having your daily feed bombarded with such messages will empower you to reduce your mindless buying impulses while increasing your creativity. Try the following hashtags:

#vintage
#thrifted
#ethicalfashion
#fashionrevolution
#fashionactivism
#ecofashion
#sustainablefashion
#slowfashionblogger
#slowfashionstyle

Check out eco-conscious brands

One of the perks of the Instagram era is the rapid rise of multiple eco-conscious brands that are able to quickly reach a pool of concerned customers. Unlike many former eco-conscious brands, the new kids on the block don't forget to incorporate quality fashion appeal into their creations.

Spread the word!

Create a fashion legacy of/on your own. Nawal Bonnefoy (*see* page 118) used to be an outsider at her office with her vintage outfits. She has since converted many of her colleagues, who now come to her for thrifting tips. What about starting a movement around you?

Heirlooms from Your Mother, Grandmothers or Aunts

I have borrowed from my mother since my early teens. Her jewellery was my favourite. A silver bracelet from her teenage years first found a home on my wrist 15 years ago. My sister Olga (*see* page 90) wears its twin on a daily basis, too. It feels like an unbreakable family bond while also being minimalist and stylish. Over the course of the years, *maman* got bored with some of her Eighties and Nineties statement necklaces. That's how I ended with a lapis lazuli choker and a leather collar necklace.

Maman says that it gives her pleasure to know that these things will be worn by someone she loves. The fact I had requested them flattered her, too, as it implied that she had made a fashion-wise choice in the first place. (Brilliant – next time, I'll ask her for that early-Noughties crystal choker I haven't seen her wear in years.)

Your mother/grandmother/aunt will probably be happy if you ask her to donate a few items to you. It will provide you with an opportunity to catch up, too. She'll tell you where she bought them, the stories around them and perhaps a moving moment she associates with them. So go on – I dare you!

Jewellery, scarves and bags

Ask for costume jewellery and clothes, though it might be tactful to wait until you are freely gifted the really pricey stuff. To look trendy with designs from another era, mix them with modern basics. Inherited items of jewellery can become your good-luck charms.

Where to pin a brooch?

- On a sweater, over a collarbone.
- On the lapel of a blazer or tailored coat.
- On the upper part of your jean jacket – why not pin several?
- On your beanie.

How not to look ten years older with a silk scarf

- Tie it cowboy style, knotted at the front.
- Knot it sideways.
- Wear it like a turtleneck under a sweater or a shirt.
- Use it to belt your jeans.
- If it's the summertime, tie it in your hair.
- Use it to cover your bag strap (assuming it's not an Hermès one).

Clothes

If your stylish relative used to be your size, you have a great source of clothing with emotional soul for free. Ask her how she used to wear the piece back in the day. What did she combine it with? How did she style it? Maybe she'll show you the matching pieces or a picture. It doesn't matter if you wear it in a different manner – what's important is the inspirational conversation.

Have an item altered

If you have been given a precious family heirloom that doesn't match your style at all, you could alter it (see Chapter 5).

Jewellery

Pieces made from precious metals and stones can be refashioned into something different. A brooch can become a bracelet, a necklace a ring…You'll keep the memory but have an updated piece. Find a jeweller whose designs you like and discuss the transformation with them.

Bags

You have been donated a designer handbag from a beloved family member…but the colour is a lovely *caca d'oie* ('goose crap' – French for greenish yellow), which isn't your favourite shade. Good news, leather

A modern white T-shirt lifts this vintage yellow jacket

craftspeople like Virginie (see page 206) can change its colour and update it in many other ways.

Clothes

If they're not in your size, have them shortened, cinched and so on…

Pro tip

Don't have any stylish relatives? Rejoice, *ma chérie*, there are plenty of treasures from other people's mothers and grandmothers waiting for you in vintage stores all over.

Heirlooms from the Younger You

While you're at your mother's house rummaging through her old clothes, explore the attic, the cellar, or simply your former bedroom from when you were a teenager. There may be relics of your own. Have tissues at the ready (for both the dust and the potential tears) and start digging. I'll make some wild guesses about what you might find (clothing-related ones only – analysing unsent love letters isn't my mission here).

Cool casual clothes

You might find jean jackets, sneakers, cowboy boots or flared trousers, which can age like a good wine. If you still fit into them, you'll discover that wearing them is cooler than travelling back in a time machine.

Jewellery

The cheap items will probably be useless for the grown-up you, though Eighties kids may find pins, which I predict will make a comeback. Chances are the valuable pieces aren't at your parents' anymore but lying sadly in a little casket inside your jewellery case. It's time to redeem them.

T-shirts

This even includes those with silly messages, cartoons or scary characters. As long as the print and shape aren't too ugly (or the message too stupid), you can save them. Oversize ones have greater potential styling-wise. Roll up the sleeves, tuck in the front…Consider the colour and the look first. There may be T-shirts in cool shades you don't own yet.

Sweaters

Layer them under dressier items and, if there's a hoodie, let it hang out. Sweaters work wonders under a tailored coat, a trench or an oversize blazer. They can also be worn over a fluid dress to undercut its femininity.

Pro tip

Precious jewellery can be sold or refashioned (*see* page 71).

Fancy clothes

Let's say you got a Takashi Murakami Vuitton bag for your sweet sixteenth and then let it rot at your parents' (ungrateful, spoilt girl that you were)…Or a satin Nineties-style dress. You'll be happy to uncover those marvels from your youth.

Rings

Try wearing a ring on your little finger, on a necklace or have it resized if it is too small.

Medals

If they mean anything to you, put them on a chain. Layer several if you feel like it. Every brand is selling 'faux vintage' ones at the moment. At least yours will be the real thing.

What about the rest?

Donate things that don't mean anything to you to charity. Imagine how the cool kids will give a second life to your old stuff. If you know younger people (or have a daughter/ granddaughter/ niece), invite them to have a look at your teenage belongings. You'll be surprised by what they find exciting ('Oversize mauve jogging pants! A plastic stretchy choker! So cool, Auntie').

At a dinner I attended recently, a friend of mine related how, among his 13-year-old daughter's friends, nothing was cooler than sporting thrifted items or their parent's old clothes.

I still enjoy wearing this studded denim jacket and baguette bag from my teens

Mathilde Clauzet

Eco-responsible and vintage fashion influencer

When did you first get interested in fashion?
I can't really date it. I would say when I
was a little girl, like seven years old. I got
interested not only in fashion but in its
history, so I informed myself by reading
fashion history books. I was even writing
little fact sheets. I've always been a real nerd
(*laughs*). I was watching every show during
fashion week online and created files of my
favourite outfits.

What got you interested in fashion?
My mother was hugely into fashion. She
was a big fan of Madonna, David Bowie,
Queen… All things pop! When I was a
child, I used to try on her heels and play
dress-up with her clothes and jewellery.

**As you grew older, did you adopt the clothes
that used to belong to your mum?**
I look a lot like my mother when she was
in her twenties, and I would say 30 per cent
of my wardrobe used to belong to her. Last
week, she gave me two skirts she used to
wear in the early Noughties.

How do you get your mum to donate you stuff?
I'm super-straightforward. I would be like
'Hey, Mum, didn't you have a long woollen
skirt your used to wear in the Noughties?
I'd like to try it on.' All the clothes I ask her

about she's stopped wearing. I remember
something she used to wear, picture myself
in it, ask her about it and she says, 'Take it!'

Do you have siblings to contend with?
I have an older sister but she's not interested
in Mum's stuff. Plus she's a different size.

**How does your mum feel when you ask her
to donate a garment?**
Frankly, she adores it. Once she told me,
'Your likes on Instagram, they're down to
me.' These are clothes she used to cherish,
and she's happy they've got a second life.
Plus it's gratifying to see her daughter
getting inspired by her. It makes me happy,
too. Besides, it's a great way for me to buy
less. She just gave me a leather skirt, which
is exactly the kind of thing I would never
buy new, considering its carbon footprint.

**Are the clothes your mum has given you better
quality than those in shops nowadays?**
It feels like it, even though she didn't buy
from luxury brands. The fabrics feel like
they were more refined. Lots of silk, wool,
leather. Even the viscose looks so much
better. Never blended; very little elastane.

**Do you find that people your age have an eco-
friendly attitude when it comes to clothing?**

More and more people around me are trying to buy less. Even when they still go to fast-fashion stores, they don't do hauls.

Do you think you have inspired people who were once reluctant to buy vintage clothes?
OUI! And I say that with a big, wide smile because that's the aim behind my Instagram account. I'm receiving more and more messages from girls who say they've begun to thrift or are digging about in their mum's closet because of me.

When you buy new, what do you choose?
I buy very few new eco-conscious clothes as they're too expensive for me at my age and with my job. But if I need new T-shirts, underwear, socks, I buy local and organic. It's easy and affordable and the things are long-lasting. Recently, I have been gifted a little bag made from knitted recycled Lycra [Sakoshe by Pati]. Isn't that amazing?

When did you switch to eco-friendly fashion?
I never was a big buyer. I come from a family where we tend to save money rather than spend it all on stuff. But I used to buy fast fashion. Three years ago, I decided to buy only locally made, eco-friendly and ethical clothes. For me, all these things are bound up together and you can't choose one or the other. My number-one motivation was my feminist activism: 80 per cent of textile industry workers are women who are often at risk of falling victim to sexual abuse, among other things.

My second turning point was the documentary *Minimalism: A Documentary about the Important Things* [2016] about people who live in tiny houses and have curated small wardrobes. Initially, I wanted to follow their example, but it didn't work out for me.

Why didn't the minimalist approach work for you?
The associated clothing style depressed me. All sleek shapes and neutral colours. There was no room for fun or creativity! It suited neither my personality nor my body shape.

How did you shape your own eco-friendly clothing method?
First, eco-conscious brands got sexier and more fun. I found little red wrap dresses and Portuguese mules that fitted my *Sex and the City*-style cravings. And…vintage. Aah…the light at the end of the tunnel! You can buy the eco-conscious basics and enjoy yourself with the vintage statements.

Minimalist gurus say the only way to a tiny wardrobe is to own only basics that work together, but I've seen how your colourful

closet is really tiny and yet somehow you manage to create amazing combinations. What's your secret?

Ah, that's funny, everyone tells me the same. When I was a student, I didn't buy much as I was broke. And I've donated a lot. I recently got rid of all my high-school 'Avril Lavigne'–style and minimalist things. I now think I've found my style identity. My ultimate goal is to own only beautiful pieces that I love.

But how do you manage to put together outfits with so few pieces?

To be honest, my Insta is kind of misleading because I often borrow pieces. For my daily life, I'm developing a colour scheme that works together. Lots of pinks, oranges, reds and greens. Besides, I own enough basics to do combinations like simple 'mom' jeans and white tees.

'Vintage... Aah, the light at the end of the tunnel'

Heirlooms from the Men in Your Life

Or stolen goods. OK, let's compromise and call them items on long-term loan. This applies to any clothes that belong (or used to belong) to a man you hang out with (or used to hang out with) – boyfriends, husbands, exes, father, brothers(-in-law), grandfathers, uncles…Here are my favourite items to 'borrow' from men. Note: Wearing men's jeans is a style disaster. There are jeans made especially for us girls, cos we have hips and they don't.

Men's shirts

Picture this – a classic movie scene. The heroine has just rolled out of bed after a wild night of lovemaking, her hair dishevelled, and she puts on the first thing to hand, her boyfriend's white shirt. Holy Cinderella, it's the perfect match! A designer couldn't have created a sexier dress. I hate to disappoint, but real life may require a bit more effort. First, not all boyfriend clothes will be *that* oversize (they usually don't have breasts and neither do they all play rugby). Deal with what you have to hand.

The cotton used for men's shirts tends to be better quality as men tend to be less drawn to fast fashion than women, preferring to invest in a few good items. And as men are often taller than their girlfriends, the shirt will probably be slightly oversize. You'll need that for your boobs anyway. Tuck it inside low- or high-waisted trousers, blouse it, roll up the sleeves, open the collar wide. There you are – as sexy as our movie trope.

You can do similar styling with men's T-shirts and sweaters.

Chic scarves

Men's scarves are usually unisex. Usually shorter, they are meant to be worn in the 'loop' style. Fold the scarf in half, create a loop, pass the two ends through the loop and, *voilà*, a neat, efficient style. You can also wear them untied, following the sides of your coat. *Très chic*.

What? You tell me that only French men wear scarves? *Désolée*.

Ties

Men are wearing ties less and less. Poor beautiful silk ribbons, forgotten in the depths of a dark wardrobe. Why not offer them a gender change? Try wearing them:

- with a shirt
- with or without a jacket
- under a sweater or cardigan.

The Noughties aren't back yet, so restrain yourself from wearing a tie over a T-shirt 'Avril Lavigne'-style. (Be patient, though, your time may come.)

A spot of simple styling transforms this men's shirt

Heirlooms to/from Friends and Sisters

Before sending those unworn gems to a charity or reselling them, ask yourself whether they could make a friend or sister happy? Wouldn't that pink top that emphasizes the redness of your complexion look adorable on your brunette friend? And wouldn't those jeans that are definitely too big on you fit your curvier sister?

Person to person

Giving a garment to someone you love is rewarding if it makes them genuinely happy. However, be cautious, as something worn out or frumpy may come across as insulting. Be thoughtful and think about your friend's usual style. If you could picture her in an item of clothing that's still in good shape, ask her if she'd be interested.

Don't just go over to her place with the item, as she might feel under pressure to accept it. You wouldn't want to clutter a friend's wardrobe

just to declutter your own, would you? Instead, casually say how you've been sorting your closet and discovered a few things that you think would look darling on her. She'll be flattered you thought of her. If she is interested in seeing them, send her a picture. Then, if all's good, meet up and pass on your gift.

Clothes swapping

Organizing a clothes swapping party is an excellent way to update your wardrobe for free with new-to-you clothes.

• Invite around five to ten guests.
• Clothes sizes don't matter as there will also be accessories.
• Guests should bring a reasonable amount of clothes that are still in good condition.
• Define what can/can't be swapped (no underwear or athletic wear, for example).
• Arrange the clothes neatly (a rack with hangers is optimal).
• Let everyone pick, try on and choose.
• Remind guests to wear underwear they don't mind showing.
• There's no need to set a rule about how many items guests should bring/go away with. They're your friends, aren't they?
• That said, remind your guests that they

should take away only what they are actually going to wear. I didn't write all that about decluttering in Chapter 1 for nothing, did I?

Poisoned gifts

How should you react if you're given an item you don't like?

If they bought it
Tactfully ask for the receipt, saying that you own a similar item or won't have a use for it. Say this even if you think it's downright ugly. That's called a white lie, *ma chérie*.

If you really don't want to upset someone very sensitive…act pleased, keep it for a while and, when the person has forgotten she gave it to you (which happens much sooner than you'd think), do whatever you want with it – recycle, regift and so on.

If it belonged to them
If the item is pretty but not your style, or you don't need it, thank them for thinking of you but that you won't accept it (blame me if you like!). If the item is in a bad condition, be clear that you're not a recycling centre or charity (try to put this nicely – you don't want to start a fight).

My gold sandals were just what my sister Olga (see page 90) needed to complete her party look

Adopting Clothing from Strangers – the Myths

Having decided whether you need something or not, now's the time to decide if you can buy it second-hand rather than new. The clothes that pollute less are the ones that already exist (*duh*). Let's debunk some of the myths that can stop us from buying second-hand:

'It smells bad'

Thrift stores have a specific smell, but consignment stores smell fine, as do clothes from high-end vintage stores and second-hand websites. The garments themselves don't always have an odour. If they are mildly whiffy, it's easy to make the smell go away. I asked Francine (*see* page 180) how she deals with this issue. Firstly, if the smell disturbs her, she leaves the item in the shop. Otherwise, she says to: 'Put the item in a basin of water with a glassful of white vinegar, a big spoonful of baking soda and a few drops of essential oil. Soak for an hour, then machine wash.'

'It's stingy'

Kim Kardashian is now wearing vintage. And she isn't famous for being cheap.

'It's dirty'

Thrift-shop clothes may have been doused in naphthalene, which can easily be washed away. Clothes from fast-fashion chains are also full of chemicals, so they too could be classed as 'dirty'!

'How about bedbugs and moths?'

None of the vintage addicts I've interviewed reported such an issue affecting a single item they've bought. Just treat your cupboard with appropriate products and you'll be fine.

'I might be haunted by the former owner'

As the author of this book, one of my duties was to investigate whether or not your vintage trench coat could be haunted. So I did an internet search and all I found was a YouTuber (with 298 views) sharing how her Forties vintage dress demanded she wear Chanel No. 5. So nothing too bad, then.

'What if the former owner was evil?'

To quote vintage queen Nawal Bonnefoy (*see* page 118): 'And what if the person was fabulous?' If you really must, you can use peer-to-peer second-hand platforms to speak to the former owners to check whether they are decent human beings or not (likely they are).

'It's outdated'

Since the Twenties, fashion has been on a loop. You can combine clothes from different eras with very trendy results. Besides, you can find more recent clothes in consignment stores and online.

'The shops are messy'

Not all of them. The super-messy thrifts are the cheapest because you do the sorting. Some are very well curated according to category or colour. Luxury vintage and consignment stores often look like any high-end fashion store.

'The size is never right'

Consignment stores are usually organized according to size. If you're shopping second-hand online, all you have to do is use the size filter tool. In thrifts, the styling can compensate for quite a bit if the size isn't quite right: tuck, roll, unbutton and belt before you decide something is not for you. If you find something you really love, why not have it altered?

'I'm not an expert'

You don't need to know all the brands, all the eras and all the designers to find gems. Go for what you like; use your instinct.

'It's too much effort'

You'll become fluent in thrifting more quickly than you'd expect. It's all about finding the source that works for you.

'Kim Kardashian is now wearing vintage'

Adopting Clothing from Strangers – the Perks

Now that we've debunked the myths on
the previous page, let's look at the perks
of buying second-hand:

It's cheaper

Nothing is cheaper than thrifts, charity shops, flea markets and garage sales. Long before environmental concerns about clothing production came to prominence, one of the main motives for enthusiastic thrifters was grabbing a bargain. That said, when you enter a curated vintage shop or fancy consignment store, you'll encounter price tags that will be more expensive than those of fast-fashion stores. However, compared to a new item of the same quality, they're usually still cheap.

It's unique

Last summer, a Spanish fast-fashion dress was worn by so many people that an Instagram page and a host of magazine and online articles were dedicated to the phenomenon. Are you sure you want to be part of that? Items that were produced decades ago have lost their siblings, so you'll get lots of compliments on your vintage treasure and its originality. When asked where to find it, you'll mysteriously answer: '*C'est vintage.*'

It has a patina

Age enhances the look of many leather or denim items.

It can be good as new

People get presents that they don't like and buy items they don't wear. On the second-hand market, many of the clothes you'll find are as good as new. On the internet, you can search second-hand clothing sites with a 'like new' filter. In consignment stores, clothes may still sport their original labels. Some shops also specialize in the retail of dead stock, which is unsold merchandise that may have been in storage for decades!

It's long-lasting

If a jean jacket from the Eighties has made it through 40 years without a hole, it's going to be around for at least the next 10 years. If you're looking for recent second-hand items, target the brands that are famous for their quality.

It's sustainable

Bah oui! That's the whole point of this book!

It's been 'preloved'

And we love to share the love.

Irma, the photographer of this book, elegant in head-to-toe second-hand attire

How to Navigate 'Bulk' Thrift Stores

The cheapest thrift stores will buy in bulk without doing any sorting and leave it to you to go through piles of uglies to find a rare beauty. Hence, the very cheap prices. Racks and trays are cramped, so you have to be prepared to do some digging and lifting. The shop (though not all the clothes) carries a peculiar smell that may bother some (*see* page 82). If you're not ready for this, and prefer fancier kinds of second-hand shopping, go elsewhere. Otherwise, enjoy! This is the place where passionate thrifters discover their best finds (and brag about it forever afterward).

How to search

Put your eyes and hands into browse mode. Feel the fabrics. Home in on the colours and prints you love. Have no fixed plan.

What you'll find

Anything and everything and for ridiculously small prices. Nineties zipped sweaters, jean rompers, Forties dresses, Eighties bomber jackets, utility jumpsuits… The list is endless.

' The place where passionate thrifters discover their best finds '

Pro tips

- It is OK to make some mistakes. The low prices make mistakes affordable, and the successes will more than make up for the failures.
- If you buy several items, try to bargain.
- Ask the salesperson when restocking day is. Show up on that day.
- Avoid Saturday afternoons: the cool stuff will be gone and the aisles will be clogged with the cool kids. Mornings are fine (they'll still be in their beds).

Brace yourself! Bulk thrift stores are not for the faint hearted

How to Navigate Curated Thrift Stores

More approachable thrift stores have developed in larger cities in the last 15 years, offering customers a higher-end shopping experience. The retailer makes a selection, keeping only the best. Clothes are sorted according to category and sometimes also by colour or print. The clothes may have some minor defects, but nothing that would make them unwearable. Because the clothes are curated to a degree, you save time, but the clothes are more expensive.

Each store will have its own identity with a unique decor, atmosphere and curation. Some are more into a specific era; others into a certain style. Find the one(s) that match your own vibe. Smell and mess are mostly absent and, even though the racks are full, it is much easier to navigate through the store than at bulk thrifts (*see* page 86).

How to search

If you've something in mind, home in on the appropriate rack. The current trends (for which, easily influenced human being that you are, you're probably on the lookout) are easy to spot. If you aren't looking for anything specific, just browse and sail towards the area that has the colours and fabrics that appeal to you. Wherever possible try before you buy (even if it's just over the clothes you're wearing).

What you'll find

The current trends with added soul.

Pro tips

• If you are in a small boutique with approachable salespeople, ask them for advice. They're usually passionate about their business, excellent at teaming up clothes and have an eagle eye for spotting your size.

• Look at the clothes from every angle in case there's a minor defect. If there's a stain or missing button and you really want the piece, use this to beat the price down.

At Adöm, rue de la Roquette, Paris, the owner Rebecca is a layering pro

Olga Guinut

Business and legal affairs in cinema

Shoes

I found them in a consignment store in Lyon when I was visiting my little sister Zoé. They were in a corner by themselves and immediately caught my eye. Just in my size! So I got them. The salesperson told me they were a prototype that never made it into production. They are one of a kind.

Skirt

It's a leather skirt that used to belong to our [Aloïs is my sister] grandmother. Aloïs took it from the 'costume box' when she was around 20. It was too long on her and she confesses to have cut it with scissors. She stopped wearing it when she was around 25 and gave it to me. (Aloïs is taller than me and she actually cut it too short for her.) It took me some time to wear it. It was lingering in my closet and then one day I decided to take it for a ride. I now wear it on a regular basis.

Shirt

I found it in a huge thrift in Berlin. The store was so big, I despaired of finding anything! Then, this pattern on a hanger caught my eye. There were two shirts I fancied, so I showed my boyfriend. He thought this one had the best pattern, but bought the other

one for himself. Now he often steals this one from me. The two of us get complimented each time we wear it. The other day, we were in the shop of an edgy Swedish brand, and THREE super-stylish salespersons asked him where the shirt came from! It was 5 euros. I didn't even try it on. I knew how I would style it: a bit loose, tucked in… Like I'm wearing it today!

Ring and bracelet (not visible in pic)

I have two pieces of jewellery I never take off. The gold ring was one of the ones our great-grandmother gave to the six of us when we were kids. It's like a signet ring 'cause we have our initial engraved on it. I've worn mine so much you can barely read the letter anymore. I think I have been wearing it since I was eight. When I grew up, the ring didn't fit anymore, so I had it resized by a jeweller. The bracelet is silver. Mum had at least ten of them…She wore them all together apparently, but lost them over the years…Two were saved. I think I borrowed it at the beginning of high school and eventually ended up making it mine. I don't recall actively asking her. Both the bracelet and ring go with everything. They're a perfect combination.

How to Navigate Charity Shops

Thrifts have been criticized for importing their merchandise from far away. If you want to buy less well-travelled second-hand items, visit charity shops, which usually sell clothes donated by the local community. Since the clothes are donated, you typically won't find anything older than a decade (there'll be exceptions). As the volunteers who work in charity shops won't necessarily have a flair for fashion, the clothes will have been chosen for their condition.

The display of the clothes is basic – sorted by categories and sometimes colours and/or sizes. The prices are generally low, with very little difference made between famous brands and fast-fashion items.

There's a big bonus with charity shops: the money you pay will finance an organization with laudable goals.

How to search

Browse the racks, spot the colours and prints that attract you, and feel the fabrics.

What you'll find

Anything and everything and for low prices. You may get a branded item for next to nothing because a volunteer has applied the standard price for that clothes category.

Pro tip

As charity shops sell clothes that are donated by people in the neighbourhood, you'll want to go where the locals are giving away cool stuff. In big cities, go to neighbourhoods inhabited by well-heeled older women.

Charity shops may not be dreamy, but they are great for recent second-hand items at unbeatable prices

How to Navigate Online Shopping

The improvement in internet platforms, smoothly bringing together sellers and buyers, has contributed to the current success of the second-hand market. For the style-savvy, online second-hand shopping is a wonderful playground to find the brands you could never otherwise have afforded or the exact shade of bag you are hankering after. But where do you start to look and how do you maximize your online searches?

Unfiltered apps and websites

Here, you can find both second-hand Primark pyjamas and Hermès bags. The bag may be a fake, or it may be the real deal and half as expensive as on a curated website. Unfiltered websites and apps allow anyone to sell anything they want for free. The (super-low) running costs are paid by the buyer. As a consequence, people post a LOT of crappy items. If you don't want to spend your evenings scrolling through an unending series of depressing pictures, you'll have to up your keyword search skills.

Selected apps and websites

Here, you'll find only clothes and accessories from reputable brands. Every item put online by an independent seller is approved by someone from the platform. Some have even been physically checked at the website's headquarters, which then issues an authenticity certificate. This level of safety and convenience entails high commissions, and these in turn raise the final price.

How to search

- Type in the name of a brand you like and browse the results.
- Look into lesser-known brands, which should have lower prices. Educate yourself about brands, by looking at the brand lists of high-end department stores.
- Search using combined filters: 'Green + T-shirt' or 'Coat + Max Mara + beige'.
- Enter different word combinations in the search bar. Think of synonyms (some vendors use absurd descriptions).
- Learn the technical terms to describe clothes (twinset, Mary Janes, raw silk…).
- If looking for shoes, filter by condition (new or as good as new).

- Programme alerts on your phone when searching for something specific.
- Educate yourself about vintage brands and search for them. You can find unique pieces for great prices.
- Browse archives of classic magazines and search for the pieces online.

What you'll find

- Medium to luxury brands at reasonable prices.
- Lots of fast-fashion. Mostly not worth it, but sometimes interesting. It's OK to buy second-hand fast fashion…but only if it's selling for significantly less than it was in the store.

Pro tips

- If you live in a big city, limit your search to sellers who live there, so the carbon footprint of the shipping will be lower. Otherwise, confine your search to your own country.
- Ask for precise measurements when you don't know the fit of a brand (shoulders, breasts, waist, hips and lengths).
- Always negotiate, unless it's a real bargain. Most sellers include a negotiation margin in their prices.
- Look at the date that the items were first put online. The longer it's been on the platform, the more likely you are to obtain a discount.
- To prevent impulse buys, create a wish list, leave it for a while and come back to it later.

How to Navigate Garage Sales and Fleamarkets

Spring and autumn are the high season for garage sales in Paris. If you go for a Sunday stroll, you'll often encounter a collection of charmingly ramshackle stalls run by a mixture of professional and non-professional sellers next to a *merguez* sausage stand. You'll easily recognize the non-professionals by the fact that the clothes on their stalls are all obviously theirs. The clothes are usually clean, having come straight out of the closet. Some are a bit worn; some are as good as new.

How to search

Don't be shy and have a good rummage through. If someone's wardrobe discards match your style, then dig deeper – you may find some treasures.

What you'll find

• Lots of cheap yet cool modern items (again, it's OK to buy used fast fashion).
• Some vintage pieces from grandma's closet.
• A few pieces of low-priced clothing of branded quality.

Beware of counterfeits!

The most famous brands are the most copied. Examine the quality of a bag and its detailing, just as you would do for a bag were you to buy it new. If the details aren't perfect (I am not talking about signs of wear here), then the bag is probably a fake. Look at the hardware, the printing of the name (which should be three-dimensional and not merely written) and the stitching. Everything should be perfect.

Prior to buying a luxury item, go to a bona fide luxury vintage shop and get to know the technical characteristics of a particular brand.

Pro tips

• Aim for the chic neighbourhoods where elegant wealthy ladies may have got rid of their Lanvin heels for next to nothing (true story).
• Or go for the hipster districts where the cool kids are in the habit of reselling their fashionable clothes.
• Countryside sales are magical places where you may find grandma's bags in perfect condition for just a few pennies.
• Bargain if you buy in bulk and if the price is more than two digits.

A temporary flea market in Paris's Marais district

Alice Mazaré

Brand manager in advertising

Cap

I inherited it from my brother's ex-girlfriend about ten years ago and have worn it on a regular basis ever since. There's a little bow on the side that makes it unique. I feel quirky, arty and a little bit 'old fashioned', and I get complimented on it a lot.

Top

I found this little sweater on Vinted. It was size L but looked like my size [Alice is 1.6m/ 5ft 2in tall]. I mean, don't get me wrong, I like to wear oversize, but this one isn't meant to be worn that way. In the picture, it looked cropped, stretchy and small. I gave it a shot – I mean, it's rare a sweater doesn't fit AT ALL. I was right, it was absolutely perfect!

Jeans

I bought these 'Jane Birkin' jeans on the same app from a seller I know who is the same size and height as me. Jeans are difficult to buy online because the fit has to be perfect. It matters if they're stretchy or rough as well. I had asked the seller for the precise measurements of the jeans. They perfectly matched mine, so I bought them, and I don't regret it. They fit like a glove. Super-comfy and flattering.

Boots

They are from Vinted, too (*laughs*). They popped onto my landing page suggestions. The heels are higher than on the other boots I have. In the picture they were shown with 'mom' jeans, which made them look very feminine. I thought that I would use them in the same way, but they also look great with these high-waisted flares.

Belt

I found it at a garage sale about ten years ago for 2 euros. As I didn't own a waist belt, it was a perfect addition to my wardrobe.

Rings and bracelet

The snake ring is a gift from my mother. I own a few pieces of gold-coloured jewellery so this one's great. The other ring has a fun story. My mum had to remove her wedding ring because she was having surgery (nothing big), but afterward she wasn't able to put it back on. She sent me on a mission to find a replacement and I found this very thin gold ring. I loved it so much I also bought one for myself. Now we have the same ring – it's like a bond. And the little leather bracelet? (*Laughs.*) Yesterday, a friend bought a bag and this came with it. She attached it to my wrist, and there it still is.

How to Navigate Consignment Stores

This type of second-hand store resells the belongings of individuals on their behalf. The clothing selection is often highly curated by the boutique's owner, who will reject any clothes or accessories that don't match the shop's style profile or reach its quality requirement. The vibe of the clothes on display can be completely different from one consignment store to another. Look for the one that matches your style.

The prices in consignment stores are based on current market second-hand retail prices. They'll be roughly the same as those on curated second-hand online platforms.

Some consignment stores feel just like luxury boutiques, making them perfect for second-hand beginners who may feel intimidated by fleamarkets and thrifts.

How to search

The hardest part is to find a store that you like. Browse the list of consignments in your area and pay them a visit. If you live in a small town, there may be only one (or none). In Paris, there are more than a hundred. There are online consignment stores that share their selection on their Instagram feed and their website. In this way, you can get a feel of what you can find in the boutique.

What you'll find

High-quality designer items for affordable prices displayed in a pleasant, comfortable environment.

Pro tips

• Become friends with the owner and let them know what you're looking for. They'll alert you when they receive something that matches your request.
• Look for quality rather than the brand. Many excellent brands are unknown to non-fashion-savvy crowds.
• Ask the owner about the clothes – they're always very knowledgeable.
• Eloïse (*see* page 107) told me a secret about consignment stores: buy out of season. The demand for winter coats is lower in mid-summer, so the prices will be cheaper and you'll be able to negotiate a better deal.

At Louise Paris, second-hand items from luxury designers become affordable

Élodie Fiers

Vintage entrepreneur

Boots

Lots of inspiration comes from the movies and vintage pictures. Up until the Nineties there were no stylists on the red carpet, so the looks were more free. These boots were inspired by a photo of Gwyneth Paltrow in the Nineties, wearing stretchy denim boots. I sent the picture to a friend who is thrifty on Vinted and asked if she could find some in a similar shape. These are not denim, but they were just the shape I was after and look great.

Trench coat

From a thrift store. It has two layers – in spring, you can remove the wool underlayer. The label looks amazing, too. I love seeing vintage labels of unknown brands. Thrifting has always been my thing. From a young age I was told to buy fewer good-quality things and not to purchase things that were produced by exploiting people. When I was nine, everyone was wearing Nike at school. I told my dad I wanted some of that stuff, too. He said that the sneakers were produced by kids who didn't have a chance to go to school like I did and refused to get me a pair. I was upset, but now I get his point. For our clothes we went to flea markets where we had to rummage to find the cool things.

Jean jacket

I bought it at the end of the day at a bric-à-brac fair. By that time, the merchants are tired and don't want to put the stuff back in their vans, so it's much easier to bargain. Actually, the two best options are either to be the early-bird and get the real gems or the last one and get some very good deals.

Sweater

It comes from a 'mad vintage' shop. They must have discovered a dead stock because there were plenty of different colours! You can tell it's dead stock because the ancient price tags are still on.

Pants

From H&M three years ago. I don't go into fast-fashion stores anymore, but I think these look great. I picked them because they had silk in them and can be dressed up or down.

Bag

The bag is an old Longchamp that used to belong to my partner's mum. She passed away and he wanted me to have something of hers. I've tied a silk scarf that I got from Kilo Shop [vintage store in Paris that sells items by weight] around it.

How to Navigate High-end Vintage Stores

The high-end vintage boutique could not be more different from the thrift store, displaying only a carefully selected range of clothes. The owner chooses a theme based on their favourite style or era. There are vintage boutiques that specialize in rock styles, others in haute couture; some carry mostly clothes from the Seventies, while others prefer Fifties pinup garments.

The boutique's atmosphere totally depends on the aesthetic choices of the merchandiser. It may feel like a spacious, high-end fashion store or be a small boutique crammed with treasures right up to the ceiling. The prices may seem high for vintage at first sight, but a good look at the quality of the fabrics and designs will quickly make you realize that it's still much cheaper than anything similar you could get new.

This kind of shop, in which everything is served up on a metaphorical silver platter, is perfect for those too lazy to search.

How to search

The hardest part is to find a store that you like, especially as there aren't many of them outside the biggest cities. Come to Paris (who needs an excuse?), research the vintage stores on offer, and then prepare to spend a whole day visiting them.

What you'll find

Amazing couture clothes from every era – from long-forgotten brands, through magnificent silks and embroidered items, to designers whose prices would ordinarily be beyond us mere mortals. In a nutshell: absolutely unique gems!

Pro tips

• Consider a visit to this kind of store as a cultural pastime rather than a shopping trip.
• You can find new products in these boutiques in the form of dead stock – in other words, long-forgotten unsold clothes that have been lingering in a depot.

How about shoes?

Vintage shoes are a no-go for many people. Personally, I don't mind someone having owned shoes prior to me, as long as their toes aren't imprinted into the sole. Consignments and high-end vintage stores often restore shoes to as good as new. Online websites are also an excellent source of almost-never-worn shoes (if you know the fit of the brand, go for it). Some dead-stock shops will have unworn shoes from the past.

At Moujik, Judith (see page 168) adjusts the pussy-bow tie for me

Eloïse Laubez

Consignment entrepreneur

When did you get interested in fashion?
I've been crazy about clothes since I was nine. That's terrible (*laughs*). My mother taught us to observe nature, the things around us. My dad was into painting; she was into gardening…so, yes, seeing the beauty of the world was important. And clothes are part of that, aren't they?

How did your relationship with fashion evolve?
As a teenager, I didn't have lots of money so I had to be creative. I was digging into mum's and grandma's stuff and creating my own look with my finds. As a student, I went to all the outlet events I heard of.

Why did you switch to eco-conscious fashion?
For my business-school dissertation, I researched what the industry did with unsold stock and was appalled by the amount of wasted items. I had the striking revelation that it was meaningless to buy this season's styles when there was so much already available. So I started going on eBay in 2005. It quickly became the main source for my clothes.

Later, as a graduate, I worked for a luxury company that produced top-quality items…

but I was flabbergasted by the amount of clothing that was being destroyed for the sole purpose of maintaining the brand's reputation, when we had put so much effort and raw materials into producing them. What's more, the employees, who could purchase from those dead stocks at ridiculously cheap prices, were drowning in magnificent items they wouldn't even wear.

It was a time when we didn't have the second-hand websites we have nowadays. I had to find a solution. So I created my consignment business to put those clothes back onto the market. I would plunder my former colleagues' closets to find their unworn treasures and sell them to people who otherwise couldn't afford the prices of luxury well-made garments. And here I am more than ten years later, still saving those beautiful garments.

You have a such a cool personal style. Where do you find these gems?
A few are from my own consignment business (*laughs*), but I have not quit online bargain hunting since my eBay years. I go on all the websites and apps where you can reach the seller direct. To find interesting

products, I recommend you regularly visit the big, multi-brand, premium websites and check out the brands and products you love. Then look for them on the second-hand online market.

When I find a piece I'm interested in, I'm very cautious. I check the label is accurate, I ask the seller for additional pictures – for instance to see the inside/lining of the item – and I ask questions to be certain there are no flaws…Oh, and, super-important, I request the item's measurements to be sure it will fit. But hey, luckily we've got some excellent tailors in this world who are able to make alterations for very reasonable prices. In the end, you get an excellent-quality item customized to your measurements that will last you a long time.

How do you keep your clothes in good shape?
Using as little washing detergent as possible is key. Only organic. Chemicals are super-damaging. I wash on a low temperature – 20 degrees ideally – using gentle wash cycles that don't crush the fibres. If you wash things too fast, the fibres will break, and your clothes will deteriorate faster. Also, it's harmful for the environment as the synthetic particles end up in the wastewater. [For more laundry tips, *see* pages 196-9.]

'I didn't have lots of money, so I had to be creative'

How many clothes do you own?
I have a lot, I must confess. But I wear them
all. I rotate them so as not to wear them out,
because I adore them, and I take loving
care of them. What I have the most of are
jumpers, which dress a silhouette, and shoes,
which finish an outfit. For instance, you wear
jeans and a T-shirt, add some wonderful
shoes and, boom, you look like a million
dollars. I wear absolutely all I have in my
closet. If I haven't worn something in a year,
I sell it. It means there's probably something
wrong with it that I can't fix.

Do you have any clothes that look similar?
No. This morning I noticed I had two pairs
of black trousers that look similar, so I'm
going to let one of them go.

How much of your wardrobe is second-hand?
ALL OF IT!

**How do you put together an outfit in the
morning? Do you sometimes lack inspiration?**
When I lack inspiration, I take three minutes
to go on Instagram to check my three fave
influencers, who dress super-tastefully yet
simply. I look at them and there's my idea.

How to Navigate Auctions

Attending a vintage clothing auction is an excellent way to purchase gorgeous pieces at bargain prices. Not to mention the thrill and fun. The crowded room, the mysterious phone bidders, the stylish older women, the tension before the auctioneer closes the deal…It's worth going along even if you've no intention of buying anything. Here's how to become a successful bidder:

1. Locate an auction house

If you want to attend the sale in person (which I recommend), find an auction house near where you live, or somewhere you've planned to visit.

If you want to bid remotely, you can choose an auction house anywhere. Keep to your own country to avoid paying high shipping and custom fees.

A few fancy auction houses allow you to bid online 'as if you were in the room' using live screening.

If you really don't have time to take part, place an order with the auctioneer who'll bid on your behalf up to your price limit.

If your aim is to dress yourself rather than to invest in collectables, try the lesser-known auction houses, or those in smaller cities

or towns, for lower-priced items.

2. Find a sale

Check your chosen auction house's calendar for the next vintage fashion and jewellery auction. Download the catalogue and see whether any lots interest you. There are? Then…

3. Be prepared to bid

Optimally, visit the auction house to view the goods you're interested in to make sure you want to purchase them. Lots are sold 'as is', so there will be no going back if there are any defects. Relax, though, as auction houses are very specific about the condition of a lot in the catalogue.

Compare the price of the things you fancy to the usual price of equivalent items. Don't take this too far, though: the right price for something you love is fixed by you and you alone. You're not a professional buyer and have no intention of reselling and making a profit. Fix yourself a maximum price for each lot you intend to bid on. Don't forget to add the seller's tax.

If you plan to bid in the auction room, show up early to be at the front where the action is. If you're bidding online, make sure you have a high-speed connection.

4. On your marks, get ready...bid!

The auctioneer will begin with a price lower than the estimate, but watch out, it will quickly escalate. To win over the previous bid, the auctioneer will generally request a rise of about 10 per cent. Raise your hand or bid online up to your fixed price limit.

Before the hammer goes down, the auctioneer may give a 'fair warning' to the room – a last chance to increase the bid.

SOLD!

Pro tips

• Go for the clothes rather than for the label. Unlabelled items are sold more cheaply.
• When a lot contains several items, decide the price you are willing to pay for only what interests you. It's not worth paying for side buys.

At auctions, the items are shown quickly, from a distance, so attend the viewing

Vintage Favourites

The following list could have been endless: imagine the task of archiving all the categories ever created since the dawn of ready-to-wear fashion…Since I have only a few pages, you'll have to make do with the trailer and hold out for the epic movie.

Denim anything

Being one of the toughest fabrics ever created, denim is the star of vintage shops. The stiffness and deep indigo colour softens with use and time. Companies do produce artificially pre-used denims…but it is a toxic process that causes lung cancer in workers. The answer: buy jeans that are genuinely pre-used.

Jeans

What to choose
One hundred per cent cotton jeans age the best and are the toughest. Elastane, that's been added to denim for the last 20 years, makes the fabric prone to tearing.

Any shade of blue, black or white, but don't forget the fun ones in other colours.

Avoid jeans with artificial creases or if you can see vertical lines in the canvas.

The fit
Anything from 501 hourglass shapes to high-waisted flares. But you'll have to try and try…Designs and sizings have been modified over the years, so a number means nothing.

How to wear
Keep them as you find them or do some minor upcycling such as cutting the hem. If they are oversize, try belting them for a paper-bag-pants look.

Denim Jackets

What to choose
Oversize, snug, sleeveless, studded or Eighties shapes.

How to wear
As they are or cut them into a cropped jacket. I love denim-on-denim outfits, either using the same or a variety of shades. Jean jackets can make pretty dresses or skirts look more relaxed.

Leather

This is another fabric that stands the test of time. In high-end vintage shops, you'll find impeccable pieces. In affordable thrifts, you may notice some scratching and fading. As long as it's not too obvious, this can add soul to the piece. There are few things that a bit of hydration and dyeing won't fix.

Biker jackets

What to choose
Oversize ones, shrunken ones... all are cool.

How to wear
In winter, I wear a sweater underneath and top it with an oversize scarf. They make dressy trousers and frilly dresses look cool while emphasizing the rock attitude of denim-based outfits. You can also wear them over fancy clothes to go out.

Leather skirts

What to choose
The pencil skirt is an eternally sexy classic. Try on a few and find your match. Make sure you can walk (and not only on tiptoe). A black leather skirt is timeless, but other colours are fun, too.

How to wear
Tone things down with an oversize top: a fluffy sweater, a men's shirt or a square T-shirt. Tuck or half-tuck to show your waist. Team with sneakers, flats, low boots...or sexy heels for a night out.

Leather trousers

What to choose
These will be mostly be high-waisted and pleated: super cool.

How to wear
With a tight or loose sweater – maybe in the same colour – tucked in. Add a belt to define your waist.

High boots

What to choose
Seventies-style straight boots or the more relaxed shapes with the triangular heel from the Eighties.

How to wear
Seventies-style boots work wonders under both short and knee-length skirts and dresses. Their Eighties siblings can make the leg look a bit heavier, but I love them over skinny jeans or with short skirts and dresses.

Belts

What to choose
The belt needs to fit the size of the hoops on your jeans or trousers, never smaller. An oversize belt could work like a corset.

How to wear
In the hoops of your trousers if it's regular-size. If it's oversize, use it to cinch a flowy dress, a jacket...plus anything oversize!

Bags

What to choose
Anything you like. Make sure the lining and straps are in good condition. If they aren't, you can always have the price reduced and do some DIY upcycling (see page 216).

How to wear
This isn't as stupid a question as it sounds. You can wear the bag diagonally with the strap across your body or with the strap on one shoulder so that the bag sits at your side. You can also carry the bag in front of your body...*Oh les petits détails!*

Workwear

As the name suggests, another super-tough category of clothing.

Trench coats

Trench coats were first worn by soldiers to protect them from the rain and mud in the trenches during the First World War.

What to choose
Older trench coats are less cinched than those from more recent decades. Luckily, the larger versions are making a comeback. Check for stains and tears in the lining.

How to wear
A trench adds attitude to anything – REALLY! Try it and see for yourself. Looks better worn open (as long as it's not raining).

Utility jumpsuits

Factory workers used to wear blue jumpsuits as utility gear – for this reason, the colour came to symbolize a social categorization,

dividing the 'blue collar' workers from the 'white collars' (office) ones. Whether it's cultural appropriation for an office girl to don a utility jumpsuit is a question I'll leave you to answer. I can only assess its potential in terms of style.

What to choose
You want to find a fabric that has 'been through the mill'...so look and feel are key.

How to wear
Open the buttons to reveal a low-cut T-shirt underneath, roll up the sleeves and trouser-leg hems, and add some heels, jewellery and a bit of makeup. Or, you may prefer to go minimalist to keep the raw feel of the piece. If it is baggy at the waist, don't forget to belt it.

Army gear

Khaki army gear were best-selling thrift items a few years ago, but interest in them has waned. I predict a comeback, however.

What to choose
The classic army jacket. This will be oversize (you're very likely to be smaller than most soldiers).

How to wear
It used to be cool to wear an army jacket over flowy dresses or skinny jeans, but I recommend teaming yours with unexpected colours like an all-white outfit or something bright red.

Classic Womenswear

Although softer than their tougher sidekicks, these items have still stood the test of time.

Blouses

What to choose

Silk pussy-bow blouses, Victorian collars, dainty lace... The details and fabrics are much more refined than anything manufactured today.

How to wear

If you want to undercut their 'femininity', forget about skirts and go for trousers or shorts of any kind – mom jeans, flared jeans, cigarette trousers, paper-bag trousers, cut-off denim shorts, leather shorts – and tuck the blouse in. You don't have to make an actual bow with your pussy bow, just tie a simple knot. Victorian collars and high-neck pussy-bow blouses work wonders when peeking from underneath a crew-neck sweater.

Pleated skirts

What to choose

I recommend midi length if your school uniform years are long behind you.

How to wear

With Seventies-style high boots in autumn, platform sandals in summer and ballet flats if you're in a Bardot mood. For an hourglass figure, tuck the top in and add a belt. For a more daring look, wear with an untucked oversize sweater and heels.

Silk scarves

Like candies next to the cashier in the supermarket – the cheap impulse buy at the end. There are usually mountains of scarves available.

What to choose

Good news – most of them are silk. And they're cheap. Feel the softness to be sure it's the real thing (*see* page 167). Prints,

shape and size don't matter – just go for what appeals to you.

How to wear

Under a sweater or shirt like a turtleneck. In your hair as a scrunchie. Around your bag handle. As a belt...The options are endless.

Embellished jumpers

Those jumpers with pearls or cute embroidery that your grandmother and French TV anchor Anne Sinclair used to wear are cool again.

What to choose

Something that's not itchy, smells good and looks pretty.

How to wear

With something either sexy or masculine – a leather skirt, jeans, chic cigarette trousers...Don't forget to roll up the sleeves and half-tuck the front.

Cool stuff from other decades

Remember when Buffalo platform shoes were cool and then they weren't anymore? They're back. Or those Galliano newspaper-print dresses? Well, they're back, too. The truth is: anything that was cool in the past is likely to make a comeback. Stack some designer stuff in a box just in case.

Designer statement pieces

What to choose
Oversize shoulders, Eighties primary colour mixes, sultry Saint Laurent fabrics… anything really bold will turn a simple outfit into something trendy. This kind of thing is easier to find in high-end vintage stores, auctions or online using well-chosen keywords. And look out for the forgotten designers. If you learn about a new one in a high-end vintage store, remember the name for later online searches.

How to wear
As always with statement pieces, mixing them with basics is a safe option: jeans for casualness; black trousers for sophistication.

Statement belts

What to choose
This Eighties favourite is a jewel for your waist. Choose whatever catches your eye (but keep in mind that you'll need to pair it with something you already own).

How to wear
With flowy dresses, oversize white shirts or large sweaters, or with a skirt and fluid top.

Massive costume jewellery

What to choose
Anything big and loud that doesn't hurt (or accept that those clip-on earrings will be bearable for only a couple of hours).

How to wear
Either use just one piece as a statement or stack them like Coco Chanel. They work with both basics and loud pieces, such as a printed silk blouse or a band T-shirt.

Band T-shirts and sweaters

What to choose
Whatever appeals to you visually. They can often be pretty ugly (like the ubiquitous one featuring a wolf howling at the moon), but they're still cool.

How to wear
In any situation where you would have worn a basic T-shirt. Layer with a plaid jacket, tuck it into your sexy leather skirt or classic pleated one, or hide it under layers of necklaces.

Shoes the same colour as the vintage bomber's embroidery complete this look

Nawal Bonnefoy

Journalist and vintage fashion blogger

When did you first get into fashion?
When I was a child. My parents were passionate about clothes and they had A LOT. I always loved dressing up. Growing up, I wanted to be a fashion journalist 'Carrie Bradshaw'-style. I wanted that giant walk-in closet with the clothes sorted by colour. I still do, but I live in a 30m² apartment in Paris with my boyfriend, so it's impossible. From a young age, I accompanied my parents to bric-à-brac fairs, mostly to buy games and books. In high school, I became a fan of *Gossip Girl*, which really inspired me style-wise. I loved their preppy, slightly retro style and couldn't find what I wanted in the boutiques. So I thought that I should look into vintage. That's how I started thrifting.

When did you become aware that fashion was a harmful industry?
Things first clicked on 24 April 2013. It was my birthday, but it was also the date of the collapse of the Rana Plaza [*see* page 162]. At the time, I was quite young and had just started working. Now I was an adult, I was excited about spending my new salary on clothes. Even if I went to vintage stores, I was attracted to fast fashion as well and was quite a big spender. I had realized there was something very wrong with mass-produced fashion, yet all that seemed so far away that I didn't change my buying habits. Two years later came a second decisive moment: *The True Cost*, a Netflix documentary about the environmental damage caused by the fashion industry. I watched it because I had nothing else to watch that evening. It shook me to my core. The morning after, I was telling everyone about it. I was ashamed of my behaviour as a consumer and told myself that I couldn't go on like that.

Is this when you stopped buying fast fashion?
It didn't happen overnight. I would stop buying for a while, then the sales were on and I'd go and get a few clothes. I was like an addict. In the end, what forced me to stay true to my beliefs was the launch of my eco-conscious blog in the summer of 2016. From that point on, I've stuck with only second-hand. Today, I can claim that I do not buy fast fashion anymore. I do not really buy anything new, even if it's from a sustainable brand, except if I really need a basic. My aim is 100 per cent second-hand…and it's cool, too.

And how about makeup?
I bought so much makeup when I was younger that I have enough to last me years – especially when it comes to blushers and lipsticks. Skincare is my new obsession.

The products have to be as 'clean' as possible; cruelty-free. I look for reduced packaging when I'm able to. I bought myself some reusable cotton pads, but I now use oil for removing makeup, so I don't need them anyway. Solid shampoo is my passion.

Fossil lipstick? But what about use-by dates?
It's funny you should ask that because yesterday Facebook brought back an old picture from 2011 where I was displaying my lipstick collection. And, hold on…I still have ALL of them today. They don't smell and I don't get pimples when using them, so the cosmetic industry is lying to us.

Where do you buy your clothes?
The best thing is always to get your clothes directly from the person who they belonged to in the first place. I come from Cannes where the yard sales are amazing as there are a lot of rich old ladies there. It's the same in Paris. Rush to the chic arrondissements. The ladies aren't interested in money; they just want rid. I've got myself some Saint Laurent or Dior for peanuts. I remember the first luxury vintage item I bought. I was 19 years old and I found a Saint Laurent wool bomber for 4 euros.

I also love real thrifts in Paris. They're a bit more smelly, I have to admit, but I swear you'll find some gems. I also love the more curated thrifts, where they stick to the current trends. If you spot a trend in the fast-fashion industry, you can be sure that they'll have their counterpart in the past. I also go to a few very handpicked little vintage boutiques where the owner has made an impeccable choice.

Do you have any advice for finding vintage clothes in thrifts?
My number-one piece of advice to my 'but I can never find anything' friends is that you should go with nothing specific in mind. If you go looking for 'a green turtleneck', not only will you not find it but you also won't find anything else. Wait for life to surprise you. My second piece of advice is not to be coy. Pull it off the hanger, turn the clothes upside down, inside out, jump into the one euro bin…What's the worst that could happen? Focus on the beautiful fabrics, the colours you like – I can spot yellow from a distance. Don't hesitate to negotiate.

And online?
Use the right keywords! As I'm lucky enough to live in Paris, where there are plenty of local sellers, I meet them directly to avoid extra packaging and transportation. If you live in a big city, search for your area. It is OK to sometimes have something

delivered. No one's perfect, and I think it can only damage your ecological commitment if you get frustrated.

Does your commitment to second-hand have an impact on others?

Yes, it's amazing. For instance, my fashion-addict parents, too, have switched to second-hand online and consignments. My father is really into yard sales and thrifts. I even converted my little brother, who doesn't care about fashion, to second-hand. It's the same with my colleagues at work – they come and show me their second-hand finds, ask me for advice…It's amazing. My friends who used to make fun of me now come to me for advice. And, of course, on Instagram, where I receive messages every day from super-cute girls thanking me for opening their eyes to the fact that vintage isn't dirty, can be super-stylish and worn by anyone, any style. Let the domino effect begin! It really has an impact.

What do you say to people who are put off by second-hand stuff?

Once there was a little grandma in the street who complimented me on my elegant outfit and I'm like, '*Oh merci, madame*. It's a dress from the Fifties', thinking she would be interested as she had lived through the decade. Suddenly the cute *mamie* turns into a shrieking witch: 'Aren't you ashamed? You've stolen from a dead person!'

It made me think. First, clothes aren't haunted. Second, maybe the former owner wasn't so good (and so what?), but what about if you took the opposite mindset? What if your dress has been all around the world, if an amazing woman accomplished great things while wearing it? Fell in love, experienced her first kiss? An extraordinary destiny? What if the clothes could share their magic with you, empower you and give you the strength to experience amazing things while wearing them?

'My friends who used to make fun of me now come to me for advice'

The Size 'Issue'

Whether you're really petite, have a tall, curvy frame or consider yourself just 'medium', you may feel discouraged facing a rack of thrifts where nothing seems to be your size. Don't despair. First of all, read this page and remember the rule of all good thrifters: oversize tops can be super-stylish. Then, turn the page to find out which second-hand styles will suit your body shape and how you can tailor thrifted items to work best for you.

How to style oversize tops

• Tuck the top in all the way around in high-waisted bottoms, making sure the extra fabric lays flat inside (be careful not to create faux belly rolls).
• Half-tuck the top over a medium- or low-waisted bottom.
• Roll up the sleeves.
• Belt it.
• If you feel like you need it, add heels to lengthen the body.

Oversize shirts
• Knot the hems to the desired length.
• Open the upper buttons and add a necklace.
• Unbutton it all the way, wrap it and tuck in for a sexy twist.
• Wear it out and belt it.
• Wear it open as an over layer.

Oversize T-shirts
• Roll up the sleeves to create a 'muscle top' (no muscles required).
• Half-tuck it over a medium- or low-waisted bottom.

Oversize knits
• Add a necklace or big earrings.
• Tuck the front over a high-waisted bottom and add a belt.
• ...Or just belt it.

Oversize jackets (tailored jackets, jeans jackets, biker jackets)
• Wear something really fitted on your bottom half.

Petite Alice (see page 98) tames her large knit by tucking it into a high-waisted, fitted skirt

Whatever your size...

...There'll be plenty of options:

If you're petite

There should be lots of options for the petite figure, as women used to be smaller in the past. Many of the smaller sizes are waiting for you like that glass slipper waited for Cinderella – minuscule jeans, super-tight leather skirts... If you have tiny feet, vintage shoes may be your answer.

If you're tall and/or curvy

As oversize was trending in the Eighties and Nineties, you'll find lots of options in the tops department. You can also pay a visit to the menswear section for unisex garments. However, in terms of very womanly and fitted clothes (like dresses or skirts), it can be much more difficult to find clothes that fit as the plus-size market

has developed only recently. Maybe in the coming years we'll see the rise of dedicated second-hand and vintage stores. Some already exist in the USA. Feel confident to ask the owner of a curated vintage or second-hand store if he or she has something for you.

If you're 'medium'

As selections are made based on what the 'average' customer will buy, you'll find plenty of clothes that fit you.

Have it tailored!

Personally, I think any item of clothing should fit me straight off; otherwise it means it's not meant for me. It's a good way, in any case, to keep down the number of your purchases. That said, if you're petite or have a very tiny waist, alterations are often needed. These ones are easy to do:
- A top too long? Have the bottom shortened to your liking.
- Trousers too long? Have the hem shortened; if they're jeans, you can also cut them raw.
- Trousers too large? Have the waist taken in. (Note: this doesn't work on jeans!)
- A top, jacket or dress too large? Have the cinching narrowed.
- Trousers, a dress or a skirt too snug? There's often a bit of room for one size enlargement.

Pro tips

- Can oversize work on a curvy woman? Yes! Recently, I styled a size-16 client with a thing for geeky printed T-shirts. Her collection was cool but her tees were tight, making it impossible for me to style them. I took her to Amel's curated vintage shop (see page 149) which always carries a selection of dead-stock oversize printed T-shirts. She came out of the changing room looking disappointed in her big tee. I tucked the front of it inside her jeans, folded the sleeves, and added a belt and a necklace. Her face lit up and she bought the top.
- To roll up your shirt sleeves, create one big fold up to 4cm (1¾in.) below the elbow. Double the fold. You're done.
- You can't make the shoulders of a blazer narrower.

The Online 'Non-returnable' Issue

Whether it is through a website, via an online or second-hand store, returns are next to impossible as this wouldn't be economically sustainable either for sellers or the platforms. It's a hit-or-miss game. To give yourself the best chance possible of being satisfied with your purchase:

Ask about the details

Make sure to double-check that there aren't any defects you may have missed by asking for extra pictures. Most sellers are usually very honest about this kind of thing as they want to get good reviews.

Ask for the precise measurements

The biggest issue is size. If you don't know the brand, ask for precise measurements.

If there's a picture of the item being modelled on Instagram or the website, you can estimate how it will look on you based on the size of the model showcasing it (which is usually provided).

Ask whether it meets your needs

When in doubt, ask for details about the comfort/practicality – is it heavy/warm/itchy and so on? Are the platforms stable?

Pro tip

Don't buy anything too expensive online unless you have an idea of how the clothes will look because you know the brand or because you've tried it on in the past.

The Age 'Issue'

'Will wearing "old" clothes make me look older?' This is something that worries a lot of my clients. Yet, I know plenty of amazing women past their forties who look fabulous in vintage, like Amel (*see* page 149) or Francine (*see* page 180) or influencer Sophie Fontanel, who is in her late fifties but rocks the bourgeois style like a queen. Here is my advice:

Get your inspiration from decades other than those of your twenties

If you are 50 years old, it means that you were in your twenties and thirties in the Nineties and Noughties – decades that are now experiencing a massive revival among today's 20-somethings. Yet, as far as you are concerned, those trends are the trickiest as you don't want to look like you haven't evolved since.

Borrow from those decades that peaked *before* you reached twenty. This way, it's an obvious homage (and not a question of you having got stuck in the past). The good news is that the Sixties and Seventies are inspiring lots of designers at the moment.

Wear jeans, cool sneakers, T-shirts or androgynous tailoring

In fashion terms, these are the fountain of youth. Next to them, anything vintage will look modern.

Wear vintage in a modern way

Avoid wearing a 'total look' from a single era. Instead, combine new garments with vintage ones or mix vintage pieces from a variety of past decades. Your look should say 'inspired by' and NOT 'I'm a time traveller'. Details like makeup and accessories are crucial if you want to look modern.

Wear vintage to suit your age

When I optimize my over-50 clients' wardrobes, I often suggest that they get rid of some of their belongings even if these happen to be totally back on trend. This is because they were trendy for twenty-somethings 30 years ago. Those same clients can wear items from the Nineties today and look amazing...IF they choose those that are age-appropriate for them now.

Consultant Martine Faye balances her Seventies padded rust jacket and vintage band T-shirt with rock-attitude skinny jeans and cowboy boots for a contemporary vibe

Martine Anjorand

Stylist

Dress

Discovering Comme des Garçons made me discover a new way of dressing yourself. I bought this dress in one of its first boutiques, in rue Etienne Marcel, and have had it since 1995. I wear it on a regular basis. It can be once a year or five years later. All my clothes are somewhere in my head. Suddenly, I find a new way to wear them, to pair them, and they come out again.

Coat

I found it in a thrift in NYC in the Eighties. As a stylist, I was always thrifting for inspiration. I chose this because of its damask wool fabric. It reminded me of the current Jimmy Hendrix style but the coat was way more ancient! Most likely from the Sixties. There were big diamond buttons. At first, I wanted to remove them, but then I thought the design was too amazing to be altered. I also thought the shape was great. A bit like a redingote [frock coat] with a martingale [half-belt] in the back.

Socks

These striped socks are actually arm cuffs from Japan. I think black-and-white stripes work super-well with the dotted dress.

Shoes

They are from Patrick Cox, an English designer who peaked in the Noughties. He always had that British spirit, which I love, and there are always lots of unexpected details in his creations.

Bag

This is not down to me. It's down to my *amoureux* who got it for me for Christmas in the Nineties. It's a beautiful, timeless Chanel bag. I don't like to wear it on my shoulder because it feels too *madame* for me. I prefer to drag it around in my hands like a naughty little girl. I take really good care of it. When I'm not using it I stuff it [with paper], so that the delicate leather doesn't wrinkle.

Style

I have my whole wardrobe inside my head. I start my outfits from a piece – maybe based on the weather or on what I have to do that day; maybe my mood. Then I build from it. It always has to be fun – that puts me in a good mood. But then I temper the look and tone it down. Sometimes I don't. The way I assemble clothes is one of my 'weapons' in life. It has helped me in my career as a stylist. I am my own business card.

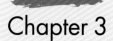

Chapter 3

The New Rules of Shopping

Buy Less, Dress Better

As a kid from the late Eighties raised in a medium-sized French city, I grew up fast-fashion free. It was a time far, far away when clothes were seen as valuable, not disposable. My mother took me shopping to the three quality boutiques that carried my (super-tiny) size. We knew the salespeople, and every purchase would be thought through carefully. Did I need it? Did I love it? As a result, I never became an impulse buyer, instead always weighing up the pros and cons of every purchase.

As a 17-year-old, during my first independent visit to Paris, I discovered two then-new chain stores, the Swedish H&M and the Spanish Zara. The clothes were super-trendy and so affordable that I could afford to buy a few items with my pocket money. Three years later, after I moved to Paris to study, those two chains provided me with half of my clothes. I was aware the quality was lower, but the price made up for it. The other half of my wardrobe was made up of the discounted branded items I treated myself to – plus a tiny bit of thrifting. Nonetheless, I never treated my clothes as disposable despite their cheap price.

Fast-forward to 2012. Zara opened in the coastal city where I grew up. The locals were so excited they started queuing outside the door early in the morning. Witnessing this from Paris, I felt a kind of nostalgia. That's what global fashion meant: wandering the streets of my hometown, I would encounter the same brands as in the rest of the world.

However, low-cost fashion had also started to make me feel nauseous. Disposable garments were a dead end for both fashion and the environment.

By 2014, fast fashion had become the default option for everyone. My former office colleagues had an ASOS delivery every week and my friends seemed to be drowning in cheap clothes. I was appalled. We all had to detox. That year, I created my blog and personal shopping service with the motto 'Buy less, dress better' as a way of sharing better shopping practices with my readers and clients.

We have to put value back into clothes, not only in terms of quality, but in terms of how we think about them. A piece of clothing is made from the Earth's resources and people's hard work. It is disrespectful to both planet and human beings to buy it without wearing and cherishing it.

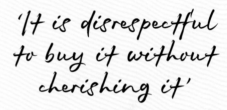

'It is disrespectful to buy it without cherishing it'

Why Do We Make Mistakes When Shopping?

Surprisingly enough, a fair amount of people tend to shop for what they already have. This may sound foolish, but it's an easy trap to fall into. Look back to the wardrobe analysis (Chapter 1). Were you the proud owner of four pairs of black skinny jeans or a countless number of similar gold earrings? You may try arguing, 'But they're not *exactly* the same.' That's fair enough, but in my opinion they don't look different ENOUGH. As a result, you'll always end up looking pretty much the same and therefore still crave new clothes… and so the cycle begins all over again.

On the other hand, you may be one of those people who buy what they DON'T have – because they want a change – but end up not wearing the new clothes because they're too different from what they're used to. Try to identify your own repeat mistakes in order to break the cycle.

Comfort zone

We are all creatures of habit. We (think we) know what works and buy it over and over. Facing endless options, we go for the familiar, with just little details that make it different from what we already have at home. It's a safe choice that you think you will wear. But the reality is that, when you already own, say, five similar things, you only wear the best of the bunch and forget about the other four.

Solution
• Look at magazines and blogs and find outfits you could copy.
• While out shopping, try on something different just to see.
• If you don't feel confident, ask a stylish friend or the salesperson to choose something for you. Trust them – it doesn't mean you have to buy what you try.

The unending search for The One

You have jeans. They fit, but they could fit better. There should be a way to get a rounder bum, right? And that black jacket you have, it's OK but how amazing does *this* one in the shop window look? So you buy it, but oh, you also need this other version that has those beautiful buttons which make it look *so* much more sophisticated…And there you are, with piles of jeans and black jackets.

Solution
• Don't settle for anything less than perfect, especially if it's a basic.
• Once you find The One, all lookalikes will pale in comparison. You'll even want to clone it after years of wear. That's what true love feels like.

Fear of the failed shopping trip

You've planned a shopping trip a month ahead. You've dedicated the whole afternoon to fill that 'nothing to wear' hole in your closet. After four hours of wandering about, you haven't found anything and start feeling bad. You grab something 'for the sake of not going home empty-handed'. Well, the plain truth is that's not going to work, is it?

Solution
• Repeat after me: 'I will shop for only what I need and what I will wear.'
• Plan your shopping trip ahead by checking out the boutiques' websites first.

Failure to think forward

Those spotted pink corduroy trousers, like bubble gum for the legs, are wonderful, amazing. You'll be a bubble of joy every day if you buy them. So you do. Fast-forward a month and the trousers still have their tag on. You have no idea what to pair them with. Even your basics don't work. Black makes no sense, your beige knit is ribbed, which doesn't work with corduroy, and your grey sweater is too cold.

Solution
• Whenever you purchase something, picture what you could pair it with.
• The pairing should be with clothes you already own, not clothes you WILL buy.

The dream of being daring

Your favourite influencer can't stop wearing brown flared jeans. They look amazing on her, and she'll wear them with anything. So, when during your lunch break you see a pair, you immediately try them on. They fit like a dream. It's a match! Fast-forward to the day after, when you want to wear them and it suddenly feels like you've escaped from the Seventies. And what will your co-workers say? No one in the office wears things like that. Having tried to combine them with every item in your wardrobe, you put them back in the drawer...where they'll stay for ever.

Solution
• If they look good, wear them STRAIGHTAWAY and go to the office in them. Who knows, your co-workers may very well pay you a compliment.
• Before buying, picture yourself wearing the item in daily life. If you can't, put it back on the shelf.

Apply the Practical Use/Style Use Rule

Our desire to buy clothes has two triggers:
• We NEED something for a practical purpose, such as smart work trousers, a light dress to survive the summer heat, a pair of flats to run around the city, and so on;
• We DESIRE something in order to achieve a certain aesthetic or, more likely, we feel an impulse to buy something on the basis of a 'love it, buy it' instinct.

When it comes to practical needs, people are generally able to think rationally and analyse what they have and what they need. The thought 'Pfff, my winter coat looks like an old rag' is followed by 'I need to replace it'. However, when it comes to the aesthetic impulse, rationality can go out the window.

The truth is: every new item you buy should tick both boxes. Take the cover-up that you need for a wedding. It has to be both practical (to prevent you from feeling chilly) and stylish (you want to be the most chic guest at the party). It's obvious enough in that situation, but all too often we plump for one or the other – practicality OR style.

If you don't apply the practical use/style use filter, you may end up with one of the following everyday 'fails':

Practical but not stylish fail

The jeans that are soooo comfy but make your butt look flat.

Dismissed!
Jeans should feel amazing *and* make you look like a goddess.

Stylish but not practical fail

The gorgeous heels that make you limp.

Dismissed!
The only place they look amazing is on the shelf; wearing them, you're like Bambi out on the ice.

Prioritize

Practical needs come first. If you need a sweater, buy one.

Style needs come second: think of how the colour and shape of the sweater will suit your wardrobe style-wise.

Pro tip

Ask yourself the following questions for EVERY item you consider buying:
• Do I have something that serves the same practical purpose (in terms of warmth, comfort, etc.)?
• Do I own something that serves the same style purpose (secondary to this practical purpose)?

Who says practical items can't also be stylish?

Shop for the Basics You Need

The styling lesson on page 38 may have revealed difficulties in creating pairings due to a lack of basics. Incorporating the required basics into your wardrobe will allow you to wear more of what you already own and therefore decrease your overall clothing consumption.

How to find the basics your style craves

List what you need

- …according to your style needs ('I need simple tops to match my printed bottoms').
- …according to your practical needs ('I need smart clothes for my job as a lawyer').

Make your basics as neutral as possible

This will help you maximize their versatility and longevity.

Stay away from convoluted cuts and standout details

These will make your clothes more difficult to combine (as well as there being a risk that they will quickly date and thus betray not only their age but yours, too).

Make your basics match your style vibe

The basics aren't the same for everyone. If you're more of a minimalist with a raw androgynous style, your ultimate basic boots may be sturdy with heavy edges. If you're a retro girl, they might be laced from the bottom to the top. If you're a rock chick, pointy boots may be your thing.

Pro tip

Make basics your shopping priority. Swear an oath that you won't buy anything else until you have purchased them.

Combine stylish basics for stylish outfits

Where to shop for your basics

Basics are long-lasting investments that are worth buying first-hand. However, if the item in question isn't subject to rapid deterioration, second-hand, vintage or thrifting is also an excellent option.

Shoes

Basic shoes are tricky to find second-hand. Go for brands that produce quality shoes, and avoid fast fashion at all costs. A shoe that will last you ten years is well worth paying more for and will save you money in the end.

Jeans

Pre-millennial, second-hand jeans abound in curated thrift stores. If you prefer a new pair, opt for a quality manufacturer and choose those made with less than 2 per cent elastane (which weakens the denim).

Trousers

Look for quality manufacturers. Men's tailored brands that have a woman's collection are a good option. It's not easy to find a perfect basic pair second-hand. If you're looking for casual trousers, try well-curated thrifts.

Skirts

Some basic skirts (e.g. leather ones) are easy to find second-hand. If you're looking for something more professional, aim for a quality manufacturer.

Sweaters

I recommend you invest in a piece from a quality manufacturer. Some new brands on the market use recycled fibres. You can ask your favourite second-hand store whether they have something for you – consider cashmere, which gets better over time (it pills at first but then stabilizes).

T-shirts

If you want a clean basic, you'll have to buy it new. The good news is that there are many eco-conscious, high-quality organic brands on the market.

Belts

Get a timeless, well-manufactured new one. Or dedicate time to finding a perfect basic one second-hand.

Why having a good foundation of basics is sustainable

- Once you own quality basics, you won't be tempted to buy others.
- Owning a good foundation of basics will increase the possible combinations in your wardrobe.
- Quality basics are lifetime investments.

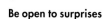

Enliven Your Basics with Statements

After you carried out the decluttering exercise outlined in Chapter 1, perhaps your whole wardrobe feels slightly sad, a bit like a butter-less croissant. If so, you've got some fun shopping time in store! You need to buy snappy items that are going to liven up your bland looks.

Be open to surprises

Your plan should be to not have too much of a plan. If you decide that red boots would liven up your outfits, you might unnecessarily dismiss that gold pair that would have done the job just as well. There's a secondary side effect of having too precise a plan: tracking down your exact ideas may prove very difficult. Have a vague idea of what you need: 'a pair of coloured boots with a block heel' is enough.

Don't be tricked into trends

Ask yourself a few questions to prevent you from buying something that will be completely outdated in a few years (or months) from now.

Is it everywhere – on the street, in magazines, on influencers' sites? If so, beware. It may be tantalizing right now, but fall flat like a soufflé in no time. The more you see an item on everyone, the more it will become linked to a certain time period and quickly become outdated.

Does it match my own style and personality? Are you a sporty kind of girl? I know I'm not, so I didn't fall for the oversize sporty shoe trend even though I thought it looked cool.

Have I seen something similar in the past? If the trend is a comeback, then it could be a good investment. Our grandmothers' leather braided shoes recently came back in an updated form. The trend was pretty widespread, so they would have been a good investment if you really fancied them.

Is the item just too peculiar/eccentric? That's fine if it's peculiar to you, but if there are hundreds like you sporting exactly the same eccentricity it gets a bit *ridicule*, don't you think? Plus it will get outdated even faster than something trendy but less crazy (think furry mules).

Can I see myself wearing it five years from now? Think harder!

Don't forget practicality

Can someone explain to me when you are supposed to wear a fur-lined mule? Think about what you're going to combine your statement item with. Even if basics are usually the answer, be sure you have the right ones to create a variety of combinations.

Amel (see page 149) elevates a basic dress with her statement bomber jacket

What About Occasion Wear?

The main reasons we need 'a very particular item' is for a very special occasion or purpose – perhaps for a wedding, a presentation or a themed party. Basically, for anything different from our usual run-of-the-mill life.

Is renting a sustainable option?

OUI for special occasions

If you need a very specific garment that you'll only wear once, then renting is optimum for you and the environment. That spectacular, high-end dress will be worn by many women instead of hanging neglected in one woman's closet.

NON for daily life

Rental companies have to constantly replace the clothes, one trend pushing out another, before selling them at discount prices at the end of the season. Add to this the carbon footprint of the shipping and the dry cleaning and it's a non-starter as far as eco-friendly options go. If you're addicted to rotation, buying second-hand before reselling or donating on a regular basis is a much more sustainable choice. Renting a piece once in a while to quench your thirst for novelty is also a good idea. But don't believe that rental will replace your wardrobe.

Costume party

You've been invited to a fancy moon-themed party. You want to turn heads, but don't want to buy something you'll only wear once. Consider the following:
- There are plenty of options online to rent costumes and dresses.
- Ask your friends if they have something appropriate that you could borrow (use social media).
- Create a costume from items you already own. A silver-and-white outfit with sparkly makeup could work. Hire a makeup artist for a fun treat AND an opportunity to look stunning.
- Go second-hand/vintage. This theme makes me think of Paco Rabanne, silver, sequins…Search online using keywords, or ask for advice in a curated shop.

Wedding

The classic situation: you have to attend a wedding and the same people who've seen your one appropriate (coral-coloured) dress five times already will be there. Consider these solutions:
- Renting is an excellent option.
- Buy second-hand. Consignment stores are full of practically new dresses (while you're there, you could leave them that coral dress). Online second-hand platforms also have a wide array of barely-worn outfits.
- Accessorize your elegant basics with creative accessories. Consignment stores are great for clutches and dressy shoes.
- Think outside the box! Trousers with a top or a jumpsuit *can* be a wedding outfit.

Afford usually unaffordable dresses thanks to rental and second hand

Buy Only the Very Best

After hours of exhausting searching you have found the black boots you were looking for. They answer your requirements: comfortable, black and chic, but the idea of wearing them doesn't make you jump with excitement. Well, I'm sorry to disappoint, but my advice is LEAVE THEM IN THE SHOP! You deserve to have a closet filled with only the best. Instead of clearing your wardrobe out on a regular basis, why not start by NOT feeding it with the 'meh' items but only the ones that are perfect? Here are some pointers to help you achieve this:

Finding The One is worth the wait

You *can* spend another week without black boots. Finding the ultimate pair will feel super-rewarding and be totally worth the wait and effort. (And we know what happens when you buy something that's just OK. A few weeks from now, you'll find yourself leering at black boots again and buying a second pair. That's bad for the environment, your personal finances and your personal style. It's a lose–lose deal.)

Don't buy something for the sake of having accomplished a task

Consider shopping as a fun thing to do in itself, not just about hefting around a full load of shopping bags at the end of the day. If you're only interested in the end-goal, you're at risk of buying something just for the sake of it. With the mindset that shopping is an enjoyable journey and that actually purchasing clothes is a bonus, the pressure will be off and the quality of your findings will skyrocket.

Pro tip

When it comes to fashion, you have to listen to your heart – that is, after you have listened to your reason (*see above points*).

Hire a personal shopper

They will know where you are more likely to find the gems you are looking for. A stylish friend works well as a stand-in. Make sure you like the style of whoever accompanies you. Some personal shoppers may not be in tune with you. It's like a shrink – you have to find your match.

Sleep on it

Not 100 per cent sure you love something? Don't purchase it (even if it's supposedly the last one in stock). Go home and let a day or two go by. Still thinking about it? Return to the shop, try it on again and then make your decision.

How to Pass the Fitting Room Test

To avoid making shopping mistakes, try clothes on in the best conditions. If you go shopping in your lousiest jeans and sneakers 'to be comfortable walking around the city', you're not going to be in the right mood. See shopping as a fun, special activity and follow these suggestions:

What to wear?

Wearing a dress to go shopping is counterproductive as you will have to remove it every time you try something on and look for a top or a bottom to match. Instead, pull out your best combination of basics along with a pair of stylish yet walkable shoes.

Avoid rush hour

Shopping feels stressful when there is a queue for a single changing room and no one available to bring you the next size up/down. Shop when things are calmer, typically mornings rather than weekend afternoons. In my experience, there's no one around at 10am on a Saturday (though maybe that's just Paris).

Assemble a complete outfit

You can't see how an item of clothing works

if it's not part of an outfit. Nothing will ever look good without shoes on, ESPECIALLY with those mismatched socks, *ma chérie*.

Double-check the size

Maybe the size you have on looks good, but what if another size were even better? You'll never know unless you try.

Always try it on

Never purchase something thinking you'll return it if it doesn't fit, because you won't.

Don't trust the salesperson

Ask for advice, but remember that they are there to SELL. Only you know what you NEED. Never forget your checklist while shopping, don't allow yourself to be influenced and trust your gut.

...But it can help to listen to the experts

This is a tricky one. Many salespeople are also style experts. Ask them for advice but keep your wits about you. Let them style the clothes on you: they'll know the tricks that will make it look good. Choose a salesperson whose style you like and admire.

Double-check the styling

Try to arrange the clothes by yourself. If you aren't pleased, ask the salesperson, your friend or your stylist to do it. Last week, a petite client of mine did not want to show me the dress I had asked her to try on, but I insisted. She exited the fitting room with bare feet, arms wide open, and the large dress I had selected forming a cross-shaped tent that fell down to her ankles. Her disappointed expression said it all. I stopped her from running back behind the curtain, shifted the belt higher, pulled it tighter, opened one more button at the top and gave her a pair of heels. A smile appeared on her face as she looked at her reflection in the mirror. She bought the dress.

Pose!

Own the clothes. Walk like a model. Clothes look sad if you stand like a scarecrow.

Move around

Sit down to see if you can still breathe. Pretend you're writing at your desk to check that, say, a shirt is comfortable enough. Put on your coat to make sure that your sweater fits underneath. Don't do those strange stretchy moves that people only seem to do in changing rooms as if they are trying to fly like a chicken. You are there to ensure that your clothes are appropriate for your daily life, not your yoga class.

Look from a distance

You want to see how an item works as part of your entire silhouette, not in awkward closeup. For this reason, you need to get out of the cramped changing cubicle to look in the larger, better-lit mirror. (Incidentally, these are deliberately included by merchandisers so the salesperson has a chance to catch and convince you to buy, but use them anyway.)

Watch other women

Outside your changing cubicle, there may be other women around. Try to analyse their facial expressions. Are they looking at you with admiration? Good. Are they reaching for what you are trying on? Very good. Are they asking you if you are taking it? Excellent. If the lady next to you is elegant, why not ask for her opinion while the salesperson is away? She'll be flattered and honest as she has no interest in lying to you.

Trying doesn't mean buying

Don't feel bad if you leave a changing room full of clothes without buying anything. That's what changing rooms are for. Don't buy something just because 'the salesperson was so sweet and helpful'.

Amel Ananna

Founder of curated vintage store En Voiture Simone

How did you get interested in fashion?

My mum used to take me to bric-à-brac sales. She was mostly looking for furniture. While she wasn't into business at all – she was the manager of a day-care centre – she was passionate about beautiful things. At around the age of 16, I noticed that, as well as furniture, there were also some interesting clothes, so I started to buy vintage.

What was your style as a teenager?

Well, it was the Eighties, so it was very loud! I liked to look unique and wasn't afraid of getting things wrong. I bought fabrics to make my own clothes even though I clearly hadn't the skills (*laughs*). Of course, I still wanted the trendy new stuff like Converse trainers or a Chevignon jacket.

Did you keep buying new clothes or did vintage override that?

It did, but it wasn't a choice. At one point I was struggling financially and couldn't afford new clothes like I'd used to. To keep treating myself, I spontaneously went for vintage. Back then, in any basic charity store, you used to be able to find prestigious brands for a few pennies. I bought A LOT.

My friends, who had no idea that the cool clothes I was wearing were second-hand until I told them, started asking me to sell them pieces. They were attracted by their uniqueness. We all want to be unique, don't we? So I sold them some. And then more. It clicked that this was my true passion, even more than my day job as a graphic designer. At 40 years old I decided to dedicate myself 100 per cent to my vintage retail activity. I was confident it would work as, over the years, I had developed an expertise that enabled me to offer a different take on vintage that focused on 'recent' finds from the Seventies to the Noughties.

Why those decades?

Because they're my favourite. My main criterion is that I spontaneously love the piece of clothing. I go for what I would like to wear myself. Besides that, I noticed that most vintage shops in Paris were focusing on the Twenties to the Seventies. The later decades were my niche! I took it.

How did you start?

Initially, I absolutely didn't want to open a boutique. I started selling online, mostly through Instagram. The problem was that, when you're selling just bags, it's OK not to try them on. When it comes to clothes you need to feel them, to experience the fit, to style them on yourself. My customers constantly asked me if there was somewhere they could try the garments on. At one point I had the opportunity of opening a boutique in the Marais. I took it, and here we are.

Do you have any advice for newbie vintage hunters?
The most important thing is to pay attention to the fabric. Then try it on! And trust yourself. Do you have a 'crush' on it? You'll find ways to style it later. If you really like it, there's a reason for that.

Is the brand important to you?
No, I don't even look at the label when searching. In the end, lots of my finds happen to have a label, because good labels did create amazing clothes. But some amazing clothes don't have a label. For me, those are the best ones.

How can you look modern in vintage clothes?
Wearing vintage doesn't mean going about in full disguise. It's the opposite! You have to deconstruct the outfit to look modern.

Will you buy something that's not a perfect fit?
Never – either it fits or else it's not meant to be. If some alteration is needed, then it was meant for someone else.

I often see you styling your clothes in different ways. Do you have any advice for those who want to make the best of their wardrobe?
Simple changes go a long way. Wear the same jacket with a sweatshirt instead of a T-shirt. Change the shoes or the bag. Wear it tucked or untucked. Belt it higher or lower. You'll feel like you're dressed differently even if you're wearing the same pieces.

How do you look cool while wearing vintage?
The secret when styling 'outdated' cool items is to wear them with jeans. It always works! Even pieces from the Thirties or Forties can be super-cool when mixed with basics. To me, jeans are the ultimate modern piece. Also, it's super-important to know yourself. Your style: what you will or won't wear. Your body: what suits you or what doesn't. I don't believe that everything is for everyone. Some clothes are made for you – you have to find out what they are and then style will come easily.

How do you avoid making mistakes?
If you have the slightest doubt, put it back, go home, and, if you still think about it the day after, go back. I share this advice with my clients and it often surprises them. If you have a doubt, it's for a reason. Maybe you love it, but the fit is so-so. Maybe you look fabulous in it, but you would never dare to wear it. Or maybe it WAS a catch. In which case, the next morning every girl wakes up thinking, 'I need to go back for it.'

'We all want to be unique, don't we?'

Buy Something You'll Wear

Even if you love something, and it ticks all the boxes, there's still one major question: will you actually wear it? Ask yourself the following questions to check:

Is it my style?

In Chapter 1 you assessed what you do and don't wear and why. If you repeatedly buy flounces when all you wear are boyish items, put those ruffles back on the rack immediately.

Is it (REALLY) my size?

Don't buy an item because you promise yourself that you'll slim down to fit into it. Don't buy tight items in order to motivate you to go to the gym. You can't know what will fit a future you. Do it the other way round: keep going to the gym and wait until you reach the size you want and THEN go shopping as a reward.

What will I wear it with?

Picture how you can combine the item with others you already own. There should be at least TWO combination options in your closet. Do this for every potential purchase, including the basics.

Will it require me to make other purchases?

You fall in love with a little skirt – it's super-cute, flattering, very wearable. The problem is you would need a tight sweater to wear with it. DON'T buy the cute skirt. Finding an appropriate sweater could take months, or, most likely, never happen at all.

Will I truly wear it?

Those shiny trousers are cute, but will you dare wear them to work or for a night out? Picture yourself in the situation: do you feel comfortable? 'I'll wear them if I'm invited to a fancy New Year's Eve party one day' does not justify the purchase.

Pro tip

Will I wear it 30 times? That's the question Livia Firth, Founder and Creative Director of Eco-Age, recommends you ask yourself before you make any purchase. I subscribe!

Avoid Making Rookie Mistakes

Failed purchases are often triggered by marketing booby-traps. Learn how not to fall for them:

Don't buy a price

You're on a shopping mission to hunt down a new pair of blue jeans. You find a pair, in all their discounted glory – half price and just the colour you wanted. You try them on. They fit. OK, not amazingly. But they're such a bargain! STOP! Don't fall into the trap! Never settle for anything less than perfect, even super-cheap items. Everything that has been produced deserves to be worn. If you don't have a plan to wear it, then DO NOT BUY IT.

Don't buy a brand

In the quality versus cheapness debate, I am a firm advocate of investing financially in your clothing and buying brands. However, a brand is not a straight synonym for quality. No matter what the label, a pair of plastic clogs will remain something without any intrinsic value. The only 'value' it carries is the branding – which doesn't justify the price. Well-established brands have a know-how they are acknowledged for, whether in leather, in tailoring or in jewellery making. Yet lots of them succumb to the temptation of marketing items without any intrinsic value for stratospheric prices. If you want to invest in a branded item, buy the one on which the brand's reputation rests. To know if an investment is worth it, analyse the quality in situ and look into the manufacturing process online.

Don't buy a trend

Unless you are sure such and such trendy item is *so you* it will become one of your staples, stay away from it. Remember what *grandmère* Coco/*grandpère* Yves said: 'Trends come and go. Style remains.'

'Never settle for anything less than perfect'

Adopt the Purchase

A purchase never really becomes yours until there's no way you can return it. Your mindset should be that no item of clothing leaves the shop unless you are sure you want to adopt it for life. Imagine the emotional rollercoaster the poor dress goes through! Don't even think of the possibility of returning an item when you buy something.

1. Remove the label

You bought the dress. You've put it through its paces, it's practical *and* stylish, you have occasions on which to wear it and you're eager to do so...As soon as you are home, you grab a pair of scissors and cut off the label. The umbilical cord between the dress and the shop is severed. Congratulations! You're the proud owner of a new dress!

2. Welcome it into your wardrobe

First, if you feel it needs it, give it a gentle wash – mmm, that must feel good after an exhausting journey from the factory or store to your home. Then find it a nice place to rest in your closet.

3. Wear it while it's good

There's always the temptation of keeping something for best. Don't do this with your clothes. The moment to wear them is just after you've bought them. A few months/years from now they may not have the same appeal. Don't shy away from wearing something because you've invested money in it. Expensive shoes are meant to be worn, providing both style and comfort to your feet. Yes, your clothes will die in the end, but that's their fate. If they pass away before you get bored of them, it means they were a good choice (and, if you've followed my advice, not because they're poor quality).

Avoid the Pitfalls of Online Shopping

If you live in a city or visit one on a regular basis, I highly recommend that you shop in physical, real-world shops for your new clothes. I know how comfortable it is to sit behind your screen and have garments delivered to your door, but with online shopping you don't have the chance to really see the fit or the fabric…which is what matters most.

I confess to having placed a few online orders. Sometimes, the clothes looked better in the pictures than they did in reality and the quality was often poor. Because I was often too lazy to return them, I stopped online shopping.

Even after years as a personal shopper, two-thirds of the selections I make for a client will be ditched due to an imperfect fit (I settle for nothing less than absolutely perfect). You should reckon on at least two-thirds of online deliveries being the same.

Pro tip

Do shop online for emerging sustainable brands that are not yet sold in store as this will encourage their development.

Buy brands you know the fit of

The easiest way to get clothes that fit is to know the sizing of a brand, because you already own items or have tried their garments on.

Don't trust influencers

Clothes may look amazing on Instagram with perfect lighting and digital enhancement, but you've probably already seen an Instagram-versus-real-life post, haven't you?

Use the zoom and watch the video

Look at the finishing on the clothes using the zoom, and, on a video, how the item looks and behaves when on a person in motion.

Check the advice on measurements

Most online retailers give advice on fit. Take your measurements to see where you belong on the size chart. If you're trying to buy from a lesser-known online brand, try to find some independent online reviews about the sizing.

Swear to return anything not perfect

Because there WILL be fails and you WILL feel lazy.

Say no to subscription boxes

The retailer's aim with those boxes is for you to keep most of their contents. This usually means A LOT OF clothes for a single person. Besides, the shipping and returns process increases the garments' footprint.

Consider the Cost Per Wear (CPW)

CPW is a budgeting tool whose aim is to help buyers make purchasing decisions. The (highly scientific) equation is as follows:

Garment price ÷ number of times you wear said garment = CPW

The more the garment is used, the lower the CPW. The number of times you'll wear a garment can be estimated as follows:

Number of times you will wear the garment per year × number of years the garment lasts

To help you calculate the number of times you'll wear the garment, ask yourself:
• How many garments with the same function do you own? (The fewer the better.)
• How many garments of the same style (and function) do you own? (One would be the best answer.)
• Is the garment seasonal? (A seasonal garment is worn less.)
• Is the garment versatile or is it a statement? (Versatile clothes are worn more often.)
• Is it for everyday or for certain occasions? (Everyday clothes get worn a lot more.)

Does the CPW method help you become a more eco-conscious shopper? Let's run through a few pointers:

Basics have an excellent CPW

As the foundation of your outfits, basics are pieces you'll wear several times a week, which dramatically lowers their CPW.

...ASSUMING that you really need them

Own seven pairs of jeans, among which are two skinny blue pairs? The purchase of a third pair will be a bad investment as it will increase the CPW of all your jeans.

Statement clothes have a higher CPW

And that's fine! As the spices to your basics, they're not expected to be worn every day. Nevertheless, they shouldn't stay in your closet for ever either.

... and an EVEN HIGHER one if they are occasion clothes

This is why it is worth considering borrowing from a friend or renting before purchasing a gown you'll only wear once.

There's no denying, then, that a small wardrobe made up solely of basics has the lowest CPW. Yet, not everyone is ready to remove every drop of fun from their closet. If you don't want to stick to basics, consider instead the AVERAGE CPW of your entire wardrobe. That way, your everyday staples' low CPW will compensate for the few eccentric finds with a high CPW.

Assessing CPW has a positive impact on your path to eco-fashion because estimating how many uses you will get out of a piece enables you to say 'no' to purchasing garments you would wear fewer than five times.

Accuracy of the CPW method

Supporters claim that this method leads people to buy fewer and better-quality items. But is the CPW of a quality item necessarily lower?

Let's compare a fast-fashion T-shirt to a well-made, organic one. Assuming that you wear each one 52 times a year:

CPW of the fast-fashion T-shirt:
10 euros ÷ 52 wears = 0.19 euros

CPW of the organic T-shirt:
30 euros ÷ 156 wears = 0.19 euros

This result is proof that CPW is not by itself a reliable method to make eco-conscious purchasing decisions.

However...

Low prices entice consumers to purchase more than they need, increasing the CPW of an entire wardrobe.

A fast-fashion garment will probably be less cared for, increasing its CPW.

A cheap garment has a short lifespan, which is more damaging for the environment than the same product with a longer lifespan, no matter whether their CPW is the same. (I own a T-shirt I bought when I was interning at Yohji Yamamoto and it's still impeccable ten years on.)

Conclusion

Buying a few quality items will motivate you to keep them in good condition for a long time, which is the key to a low CPW.

What is the True Cost (for You)?

I often hear people saying they cannot afford to switch to eco-friendly fashion consumption. Looking at the small picture, compared to the low cost of fast-fashion garments, all eco-conscious alternatives seem ridiculously overpriced. But being eco-friendly is more about buying less than about buying better. The most unsustainable thing about fast fashion is the massive quantity of clothes that consumers acquire. Consuming the same amount in the form of eco-friendly products would not improve things at all. No matter how virtuous a garment is, it still has a carbon footprint. The least polluting garment is the one that already exists – whether it's in your own wardrobe or in someone else's.

The perfect eco-conscious shopper should, in order of priority:

1. Shop less

Even people with little to spend will buy more cheap clothes than they actually need. We ALL have the ability to buy less. Most of us could function perfectly well for two years with what we already own.

Buying fewer clothes saves money.

2. Shop vintage/second-hand and swap or borrow whenever possible

In thrifts, charity shops, garage sales and on second-hand clothing apps you will find incredible bargains that beat even fast-fashion's lowest prices. Curated vintage stores feature higher price tags that match the quality of the items.

Shopping vintage saves money overall and borrowing is free.

3. Opt for eco-friendly, local and ethical brands when buying new

Yes, the cost of an eco-friendly, local and ethical product is three to four times more than its fast-fashion equivalent, but its CPW (*see* page 156) will roughly be the same, so a few years after purchase your total expense will be the same. Besides, with all the money you've saved buying less, you can now afford organic T-shirts and undies.

Opting for eco-friendly, local and ethical brands costs the same.

4. Treat yourself to a luxury purchase

Luxury brand items stand the test of time and will be cherished for many years.

Pass these pieces on and they will become the vintage for the next generation.

Time and the Eco-conscious Shopper

Time is money, as people say, though
I prefer to think of time as a valuable
personal resource we should use for things
we enjoy. So, is being an eco-conscious
shopper a good use of your time?

Buying less saves time

If you're buying fewer
items, it stands to
reason that you're
going shopping
less, going online
less and thinking
about potential new
purchases less. Spend
that time instead
thinking about how
you can make better
use of what you
already have.

Switching shopping habits demands time...at first

Finding your trusted
brands, figuring out
how to navigate
second-hand apps,
discovering the
vintage stores that
match your style and
budget all take quite a
lot of time. Once you
have it all figured out,
though, shopping will
be just as easy as it
used to be.

Eco-conscious shopping can become a hobby

Hobbies don't 'take
up' your time because
they're fun. Unlike just
buying readymade
outfits, shopping for
a mix of vintage and
eco-conscious brands
is a creative activity
in which you can get
really involved.

'Switching to eco-friendly fashion consumption will save both your money and Earth's resources'

Chapter 4

Quality is Queen

A Lesson in Sustainability

During a shopping spree with my high-school friends, I saw something I loved in a cheap French chain and asked my mother whether I could buy it. She refused, because, she said, the clothes were 'too low-quality'. I bought it anyway, but she was right. Since the rise of fast fashion in the late 1990s, the quality of clothes has been steadily declining. Simultaneously, the trend rotation has accelerated and, conveniently for the fast-fashion industry, such clothes hardly outlive the trend.

The elephant remained in the room for a few years: this ever-growing production of clothes had to have side effects. In 2013, the collapse of the Rana Plaza in Bangladesh was a wake-up call: people were dying because of fast fashion. In 2015, the documentary *The True Cost* revealed the devastating impacts of fast fashion on the Earth. It had been staring us in the face all along but no one would take responsibility for it, let alone do anything about it.

Since then, brands around the world have claimed to have improved the sustainability of their production process as well as the working conditions of workers. According to the Greenpeace Detox Campaign, most indeed have, but it's not enough. Even if the carbon release inherent in the production of a garment is reduced, if the world keeps on producing a rising number of such garments year on year, lowering the carbon footprint will have no effect. The only way to make the fashion industry more environmentally virtuous is for it to produce less. To slow down the crazy onward rush of trends and to make items long-lasting again.

Nowadays, fashion weeks create new trends six times a year. Many fast-fashion chains change their collections every week. With such a high rate of perceived obsolescence why even care about longevity? We have forgotten the value of quality. On Instagram, only the look matters. After a few wears, the piece has been 'seen' too much and people swipe to the next one. Among the items in my wardrobe are a dress from the late Eighties and a cotton jumper that used to belong to

'We have forgotten the value of quality'

my mother. They were by no means luxury items at the time, but the quality was and still remains impeccable. Two years ago, I purchased a dress from a well-known mid-price brand. It wasn't cheap but it quickly pilled and the stitching came undone.

Luckily, voices against disposable fashion are being raised among the new generation. In 2019, when a French celebrity YouTuber posted a video of her haul of fast fashion, it generated hundreds of comments from her own fans arguing that she should buy fewer clothes and consider second-hand options. Older generations, meanwhile, are feeling nostalgic for well-made clothes. To meet the demand for quality items, young brands producing locally manufactured, well-made clothes are emerging all around the world, putting craft skills back into the spotlight.

The sustainable shopper should be able to invest in pieces with a long life expectancy. This, however, requires being educated about how clothing is made – the fabrics, the techniques and the details. We will begin with the all-important fabrics and the sustainability implications of each kind.

Wool

Wool is the name given to the textile fibre harvested from sheep, goats, rabbits and other animals and has played an important role in clothing for thousands of years. Wool has a warmth and breathability that no synthetic fabric has yet been able to match.

What makes a good wool?

In general, we can say that the longer and thinner the fibre, the more refined the wool. However, each type of wool has its own properties. For a weather-resistant coat, choose a thicker wool; for an elegant, soft, warm jumper, long silky cashmere fibres are best, and for a light summer sweater, choose the breathable fibres of Merino wool. Blends that combine the properties of different wools can be excellent.

To create a coat both sturdy and luxurious, wool can be mixed with a percentage of cashmere.

What are the different wools on the market?

Sheep's wool
Sheep breeds that are not Merinos (*see below*) produce thicker-fibred fleeces and are ideal for coats.

Merino wool
Derived from the fibres of the eponymous breed of sheep, this is the finest sheep's wool and is perfect for sweaters.

Cashmere
Obtained from the pashmina goat and other goats of South Asia, this is considered the finest of wools as it has the longest and thinnest fibres. It, too, is perfect for sweaters.

Mohair
This is made from the Angora goat (not to be confused with the Angora rabbit – *see below*). It is very light, shiny as silk, and warm and fluffy. As it is prone to shedding, it's better when blended with other fibres.

Alpaca
Harvested from the eponymous animal, this is as thin and luxurious as cashmere, but more hardwearing. Again, it's perfect for sweaters.

Angora
This is made from the hair of Angora rabbits. It is very fine and fluffy and prone to shedding.

So I just have to read the label?

No, that's not enough. For example, all cashmere wools are not created equal. Cashmere goats produce both cashmere itself (made from very thin hair) and wool (made from the thicker fibres). The best cashmeres should be made from only the finest hair. Depending on how the herd is raised, how the hair is treated and how it is processed, the quality of the cashmere will be different. The less mechanization and the slower the process, the better the cashmere. Cashmere's quality also depends on its weight, so the simplest way for a manufacturer to reduce the cost of a garment is to make it lighter…which degrades its quality. That's how you end up finding cashmere sweaters in fast-fashion chains costing less than a quarter of expensive ones. The labels both say '100% cashmere', but the quality of each has nothing in common.

This observation is true for all other wools. Fibres that have been harvested and processed carefully will result in a quality product, which results in a higher price.

How can I tell if the quality is good?

Feel it, observe its lustre and find out about the brand.

Are some wools more sustainable than others?

A single sheep's fleece will provide enough wool for 15 sweaters, whereas you need to comb 2 goats for a single cashmere sweater. If you wear your cashmere sweater for 15 years, you could argue that the harvesting of those 2 goats' hairs has been justified.

What about animal welfare?

Sheep
The shearing of a single sheep takes a few minutes and is done once or twice a year. Shearing is a necessary process for the sheep's wellbeing (enter 'unsheared sheep' in your search bar to see what I mean).

Alpacas
These get shorn in a process similar to sheep (*see above*).

Goats
Cashmere goats shed their hair naturally once or twice a year. The farmer harvests the shedding hair by hand-combing the animals.

Rabbits
Angora rabbits' wool cannot be collected on an industrial scale. The rabbits endure dreadful suffering while their hairs are plucked. NEVER buy a garment incorporating Angora wool.

Can I buy woollen items second-hand?

YES! You can find excellent quality second-hand wool garments.

Pro tip

The thicker the hair strands, the itchier the wool. Choose fine hair if it is to be next to your skin. Try it on to be sure. Your winter coat doesn't need to be extra soft.

Cotton

Used in ancient Mesopotamia, Greece and Rome, cotton (harvested from plants of the genus *Gossypium*) conquered Europe from the 17th century as a competitor to local crops such as linen and hemp (*see* pages 170–1). Despite attempts to limit imports in order to protect regional textile production, owing to its softness, cotton rapidly made its way into the wardrobes of the wealthy before becoming democratized.

What cloths are made out of cotton?

Weaves
Muslin, batiste, chambray, poplin, gabardine, denim, flannel…Each cotton weave has a different style, fit and use. But more important than knowing about these is the quality: the feel and look of the cotton is what's important.

Knits
Jersey is the most widely used. Different knitting techniques are used to create various styles.

Lace
This is a beautiful fabric mainly used as an embellishment.

What makes for a quality cotton?

Some cotton varieties produce longer fibres. The longer the fibre, the better the cotton. Cotton quality depends on the production process. Poor mechanical harvesting and toxic chemicals diminish the quality of the fibres. Quality cotton has a price.

Should I buy organic?

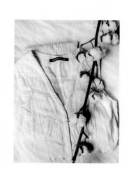

Cotton is the most water- and pesticide-consuming of all crops. According to WWF (World Wide Fund for Nature), 2,700 litres of water are needed to produce a single T-shirt – that's enough to sustain 1 person for almost 3 years. Conventionally grown cotton uses 16 per cent of the world's pesticides while using only 2.5 per cent of the world's arable land. For all these reasons, I recommend that you avoid traditionally grown cotton. Nowadays, a wide range of eco-conscious brands produce basics made out of organic cotton. This doesn't use genetic modification, is pesticide free, lets the soil breathe, uses less water, allows other vegetation to grow in its vicinity and undergoes only non-toxic treatments during the production process.

Silk

Made from the cocoons mostly of the mulberry silkworm (*Bombyx mori*), silk was first produced in China around 6,500BCE. Introduced into Europe in the early medieval period, silk seems to have been manufactured in Constantinople during the Byzantine Empire and, by the 11th century, in Italy (notably in Lucca) and later in France (around Lyon). Production is now, once again, almost entirely based in China.

What are the different kinds of silk?

Classic silk

Once the sericin (the glue that holds the cocoon together) has been removed, the silk filaments are twisted together to create a yarn that is is smooth, shiny and hardwearing.

Raw silk

The process is the same as for classic silk but the sericin is retained, giving the yarn a bumpy texture.

Spun silk

Made from broken fibres that are twisted together, this silk is of a lower quality and is often used in cheaper garments.

Wild silk

Produced out in the wild (i.e. not cultured) by species of silkworm other than *Bombyx mori*. The empty cocoons are harvested after the moths have left them, breaking the filaments in the process. The yarn is stiffer and rougher.

What cloths are made out of silk?

Silk satin

Satin is a type of weave that makes the best out of the shine of silk. It is the most common silk fabric and has one side that's shinier and softer than the other.

Silk muslin

This has an extremely light, wispy weave.

Twill

This diagonal weave is often used for ties.

Is there an organic alternative?

Yes, but it is a relatively recent development. The quantity produced is extremely low and it is quite hard to track down. Organic silk comes from the cocoons of silkworms reared on pesticide-free mulberry trees, and the silk is manufactured using a chemical-free yarning process.

Is silk hardwearing?

An 1840 article in *The Times* reported on the recovery of silk garments from a boat that had sunk in 1782. Pretty much sums it up.

What about animal welfare?

Because an emerging moth would break the cocoon filament, the larva is killed in the cocoon by steam or hot air at the chrysalis stage. You need 6,600 cocoons to obtain 1kg of silk. Whether you consider this animal cruelty is up to you.

Judith Prigent

Artist and vintage shop owner

Dress

I bought this 100 per cent silk dress on Vinted from a lady who got it from her grandma, I think. It's obviously homemade in a very pretty silk with a wacko print you never see anymore. There is no label. I typed 'long silk dress' on the app and I scrolled. That's the trick on those apps – you make a very wide search, then scroll while watching a silly show on TV. That's how you find the great stuff.

Belt

I found it at a garage sale. It's a YSL with inserted diamond-shaped parts. Typical of the early-Eighties YSL style. It no longer had a buckle, so the seller was giving it away for 7 euros, as a collection piece I guess. I sewed on the buckle from a belt I wasn't using – *et voilà*. I am not crafty, but it was easy-peasy. If I have to do something more difficult, I'll get help from a professional mender. It's always cheaper than buying new. This is my lucky belt. The other week I had a gallery opening [as well as being the owner of vintage store Moujik Paris, Judith is also an artist] to which I wore it with an oversize white shirt and black trousers. It was the highlight of my outfit.

Boots

They came from Guerrisol [a thrift in Barbès, Paris] six years ago. I had just arrived from my provincial town to study at the École des Beaux-Arts [Paris School of Fine Arts] and was very excited about this thrift store. I was going there every day, I think (*laughs*). It was just next to where I lived. The boots were so Catwoman I had to get them! They were as good as new but the heels were actually hollow. I had them fixed, and here they are. The boots cost me 15 euros, plus 15 euros for the cobbling. They are by an excellent Swiss brand, Bally, and have remained in perfect condition ever since. They're so versatile. Sometimes I wear them with skirts to show off their height; sometimes under trousers.

Linen

Linen is made from the fibres of the flax plant (*Linum usitatissimumis*) and evidence for its use as a fabric dates back to 30,000 years ago: archaeologists have found spun, dyed and knotted flax fibres from this time in a cave in Georgia, in the Caucasus region. Long before the textile market became global, Europeans dressed in cloth made from what they had to hand – largely, flax and hemp (*see opposite*). Nowadays, 80 per cent of the world's production comes from France and Belgium where the climate is ideal for growing flax. However, the raw material is often processed elsewhere.

Is linen sustainable?

Yes! Growing flax in its native environment (moist oceanic climate) does not require any artificial watering and uses five times fewer pesticides than conventionally grown cotton. However, flax is often turned into yarn in China, which entails transportation, and chemicals are used in the production process. Organic linen production is developing.

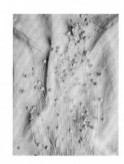

Pro tip

The higher the quality of the linen, the less wrinkle-prone it will be.

What cloths are made using linen?

Blends

Linen's stiffness makes it hard to work with, so it is often blended. Cotton (for its softness) and linen (for its lightweight strength) are often woven together, as are linen and silk, in which silk's refinement balances the casualness of linen while helping it to acquire a better shape.

Linen weave

Just like cotton (*see page 166*), linen can be woven in a variety of ways, the most popular being cambric.

Linen jersey

This soft mesh fabric can be used for T-shirts or sweaters.

How do I style linen?

Perfect for hot days. Choose a loose fit and don't worry about the wrinkling – it is part of it's natural charm.

Why isn't linen more widely used?

Linen is lightweight, summery and hardwearing, but its stiffness makes it prone to wrinkling, which caused its decline in the textile industry. Increasing environmental concerns and the growing love for a raw aesthetic, means the trend is going into reverse.

Hemp

Nettle

Like linen (*see opposite*), hemp, made from the plant *Cannabis sativa*, is one of the most ancient European textiles – no doubt visions of monks in cassocks and peasants toiling in fields spring to mind. Nowadays, it's barely used, people picturing it as a fibre only good for barefoot hippies to dress in. Crucially, too, it is complicated and therefore expensive to process, and is very stiff.

Yep, you read that right. The common nettle (*Urtica dioica*) can be transformed into a soft fabric. However, the plant is barely being farmed anymore. Formerly one of Europe's most widely used vegetal fabrics, it became completely obsolete with the importation of cotton and silk. Nettle fibres were used to make soldier's uniforms during the First World War, and today a few European companies are making nettle-based textiles.

Is hemp sustainable?

Damn, yes! Grown in its natural environment (temperate moist climate), it does not require any additional watering or pesticides. An added bonus it that it absorbs 15 tonnes of carbon dioxide per hectare, 5 times more than an equivalent area of rainforest.

Can I smoke it?

You can, but you'll just get a headache.

Could we reintroduce it in today's clothing?

Denim – which took its name from the French city of Nîmes (*serge de Nîmes*), where it was first manufactured – was originally made from hemp. Atelier Tuffery, a French jeans manufacturer established in 1893, has revived hemp denim and it looks amazing. The fibre is more hardwearing than cotton and could be used to produce lifelong-lasting denims.

Is nettle sustainable?

Yes! It grows easily in temperate humid regions like the north-east of France and could be rehabilitated as part of a re-localization process (so that the crops are processed close to where they are grown).

Can I smoke it, too?

No, but it makes a nice soup – *potage aux orties* is delicious.

Could we reintroduce it in today's clothing?

Sure. It is soft and very hardwearing.

Leather

Leather is the skin of animals that have been raised primarily for their meat, making leather perhaps the world's oldest recycled by-product. We all know meat consumption is harmful to the environment and, the eco-conscious reader that you are, you will have already reduced your animal protein consumption. Nevertheless, unless every human suddenly turns 100 per cent vegan, leather will remain a biodegradable by-product that it would be a waste not to use.

How polluting is the leather industry?

Turning animal skin into leather demands a lot of energy and chemicals. However, thanks to the campaigns of environmental organizations like Greenpeace, new regulations have reduced the impact of chrome tanning – the most efficient and effective tanning process, using chromium(III) sulphate. Vegetable tanning is still much less harmful.

How about vegan alternatives?

Most are made from oil, which, obviously, I do not recommend, as this means they are not biodegradable.

Some vegetal leathers made out of pineapple skin or apple skin have been developed. Check them out.

Luckily, more and more shoe brands are seeking out plant-based or more eco-conscious alternatives to leather. For instance, the French brand Veja creates sneakers using recycled plastic, inducted cotton canvas or rubber.

For bags, there are plenty of canvas options available.

Wood-based Fabrics

In 1884, Count Hilaire de Chardonnet, aiming to obtain a fabric similar to silk at a cheaper cost, had the idea of chemically modifying cellulose (aka wood pulp) in order to obtain filaments. His 'artificial silk' met with great success and became known as viscose. Today, many cellulose-based fabrics are used to create a substantial proportion of global clothing production.

What are the characteristics of these fabrics?

They are very soft and smooth, are similar to silk and do not wrinkle. The downside is that the extreme smoothness can make the fabric seem lacking in depth. The latest cellulose fabrics are breathable and less prone to shrinking.

Are cellulose-based fabrics sustainable?

This depends on the sustainability of the forests from which the wood is taken and on the chemical process used to turn the cellulose into filaments.

What are the different cellulose-based fabrics?

Viscose
Chardonnet's invention has been widely criticized because of the highly toxic chemicals its production releases into nature, yet it remains the most widely used.

Lyocell
This is the eco-conscious alternative to viscose. Only the chemical process differs: Lyocell uses non-toxic chemicals in a closed loop. The company that produces it uses eucalyptus wood from sustainable forests.

Modal
This is much the same as Lyocell but is made from oak cellulose.

Cellulose acetate
The production of this overly shiny fibre involves considerable amounts of toxic chemicals and has now been largely abandoned.

Are these fabrics long-lasting?

Good-quality ones definitely are, judging by the amount of viscose fabrics in thrift stores.

Recycled Fabrics

To meet the rising demand for eco-conscious clothing, the textile industry is developing patented new fabrics whose base materials are sometimes surprising.

Fibres from industrial waste

During the production processes, many industries, including the fashion industry, create waste products that other companies are able to recycle.

Fabric off-cuts

Italian company Re.Verso gathers cashmere off-cuts from companies all over Europe before sorting them by colour and spinning them into yarn again. Similar processes exist for many other fabrics.

Waste products

Formerly, during cotton production, the cotton linter – the short fibres that cling to the cottonseeds – was discarded. Now it is chemically processed using a copper oxide solution to create a fibre similar to modal (*see* page 173). This fabric goes under the name Cupro.

Recycled synthetic fabrics

The planet is being overwhelmed by petroleum waste by-products and plastic waste, so we might as well do something positive with them.

Repreve

This super-eco-conscious company has already turned 14 billion plastic bottles into fabric. It takes ten bottles to make one bathing suit.

Econyl

This regenerated nylon is made out of 100 per cent recycled fibres from abandoned fishing nets and other nylon waste.

Fibres from recycled clothes

A small percentage of donated clothes are recycled into new, raw fibres that are used to create new garments (among other things). There aren't specific names for such fabrics, but companies who repurpose recycled clothes proudly display the fact on their websites. Examples in France include the French brand Hopaal, whose workshop in the Loire region yarns old clothes into new fibres, and Chaussettes Orphelines, which transforms 'odd socks' into a cosy yarn (minus the smell).

Pro tip

Eco-conscious manufacturers like Econyl and Repreve display the brands that use their fabrics on their websites. Having a look at these is a good way to discover apparel companies who are taking their environmental credentials seriously.

Polyester and Other Synthetic Fibres

Polyester is the most-used fibre in the textile industry: 45 billion tonnes were produced in 2018…a third more than cotton with its 26.7 billion tonnes. The problem with polyester, of course, is that it is made from oil – as, indeed, are other fabric fibres such as elastane or nylon. A grand total of 50 billion tonnes of oil-based fibres were produced in 2018.

Contrary to what we might think, oil-based fibres have been around for quite a while. In 1938, the US company DuPont de Nemours invented nylon, the first ever synthetic fibre. Thanks to their low cost and technical properties, synthetic fibres were wildly successful and their production and use have continued to expand ever since.

Where are synthetic fibres used?

Everywhere…Even in the clothing of brands that advertise how concerned about the environment they are.

Are they plastic?

Polyester and other oil-based fibres are plastics and non-biodegradable. Each time polyester or nylon clothes are washed, they release microparticles of plastic that travel out of your washing machine and into the ocean.

Do synthetic fibres improve the lifespan of clothes?

Paradoxically, there are upsides to using polyester and its ilk. As with all natural things, vegetal and animal fabrics are not entirely stable: they are prone to shrinkage, abrasion and wrinkling, and they can lack elasticity. Synthetics were invented to solve all those problems and have led to some wonderful innovations in the fashion industry. Without them, there would be no transparent tights, no skinny jeans or raincoats. Moreover, when added into blends, polyester makes garments last longer – an environmental plus. However, the big environmental minus here is that it is non-biodegradable.

Is there a way to go synthetic-fibre free?

Personally, I would be very sad to have to do without transparent tights. For the purpose of this book, I searched and found just one hosiery brand (in Denmark) that creates sexy tights by recycling plastic bottles. It's a start…but a good example of how hard it is to cut free from oil-based clothing. Not every company has the time or money to research alternatives.

The Devil is in the Detail

As the English saying goes, 'The devil lies in the detail' (and often doesn't wear Prada), so, before purchasing an item of clothing, you should examine it *sous toutes les coutures*, as the French say – from every angle.

Seams and stitches

The seams should lie flat, with no twisting or bulking. Wrinkles or pulling around seams, is a sign of bad quality.

The stitches should be dense, with a MINIMUM of five per centimetre.

Overcast stitching is often found in low-quality clothes whereas a French seam says quality (ironically, the French call it *une couture anglaise*, or 'an English seam').

A flat-fell seam is expected on jeans and other garments that need strength.

Invisible seams provide an elegant finish.

Look inside your garment: are the edges of the fabric raw cut or are they finished with a seam bias? If the latter, that's an indicator of high quality. The seam will remain stable and won't rub against the skin. If an item looks messy inside, with loose threads running amok, it is very likely poor quality.

Buttons

Material

If you buy new, prefer a biodegradable material – metal, corozo, mother of pearl, wool, resin, fabric…Plastic buttons can look good or very cheap. They are fine on second-hand items.

Sewing

Buttons are better secured with a cross or a *zampa di gallina* stitch (which cannot be done with a machine) than with a parallel stitch, and they shouldn't move about on a new item.

Buttonholes

These should look clean and sharp.

Style

As far as the basics are concerned, buttons should not stand out unless they are part of the design, as in Agnès B's iconic snap button cardigan. Otherwise they can make a strong statement as they often do in Eighties outfits or on Victorian-inspired high collars.

Pro tip

When considering the purchase of a new garment, the essential thing is to make sure it looks clean and even in terms of its construction, both outside and inside the garment. You'll quickly learn to see when something's amiss.

Clean buttonholes indicate fine quality

Lining

Do not buy a coat or jacket unless it's lined. The exceptions are some mid-season coats, where it's OK not to have a lining.

In tailored, winter trousers, lining is a sign of good quality. The same goes for dresses and fitted skirts and shorts.

Avoid synthetic linings – not only is it bad for the planet (*see* page 175) but polyester will make you sweat and smell (and that, *ma chérie*, is certainly not stylish). Viscose is the most widely used lining, and it's very difficult to avoid it for now. Other cellulose-based linings are better (*see* page 173).

Silk used to be widely used as a lining but is too fragile for this purpose, as it wears and tears easily.

Zips

Avoid plastic zips and look for metal ones. The world's most renowned brand is the Japanese company YKK, the sentiment of whose slogan 'Little parts, big difference' I totally concur with. You'll find its initials written on the pull-tab.

Unless it's a feature of the design, the zip should be invisible under the fabric.

Prints

Prints should line up where the pieces of fabric are sewn together. For example, if there's a stripe on your Breton top, it should pass straight from the body onto the arm.

Three-dimensional prints (those you can feel under your finger) will peel after time. When vintage, this can give them some cachet though.

High-end second-hand items with amazing textures of high-quality wool and suede

Francine Monzemba

Accountant and thrift fashion blogger

When did you first become interested in fashion?
When I was a little girl, I loved the style of the women on TV. Then, there were the magazines...Unfortunately, the clothes were way too expensive. I dreamed: 'One day maybe.' As a teenager, I mostly inherited my clothes from my sisters: there were six of us!

Has your family influenced how you dress?
Sure. The Congolese have a big reputation when it comes to style. They were inspired by the old Italian way of dressing – really over the top. My uncles and aunts dressed up for every occasion, whether it was going to church or to do the grocery shopping. They were wearing brands, displaying the logos, wearing the latest fashions...They valued beautiful things. Besides, when they invested in something, it was a lifelong love. They weren't buying things so that they could just gather dust in the wardrobe. If today I ask my aunt, 'Show me that 1994 Kenzo bag', she'll grab it instantly. And if there was a money issue, there was always the *Mont-de-piété* [a state-owned pawnshop]. This love for beautiful things got me into trouble (*laughs*). When I was finally able to buy myself a luxury bag, I splurged on a Dior saddlebag, which I paid for using several cheques. Some of them bounced... *Oh là là.* Still, I dug myself out of it!

Did you keep spending a lot on clothes?
Sure. At the time, I was drowning in clothes. It always felt like I didn't have enough. Maybe this was a reaction to my childhood, when I never had my own things. Some of my friends were thrifting in Montreuil [Paris suburb that's home to a flea market], but that didn't appeal to me at all.

That's surprising, because I'm here meeting you as you are now – a thrift style icon. When did that shift happen?
I had a neighbour who was gifting me things and she was telling me that I should go thrifting for cheaper options, but I was thinking, 'Yes, I know, but I don't want to do that. I need new clothes for myself.' I was sick of getting second-hand goods. When I became a mother, I decided to give thrifting a try. I went to the Clignancourt flea market. I found a jacket, a dress, a pair of jeans...And it was sooo cheap! I thought, 'Hey, I'll do this again.' At first, it was a way of spending less, then I realized that the quality was way better as well.

And you got caught up in it?
Completely. That's my way of life now! Even if once in a while I fancy something at Zara, I don't buy it. I give myself a month to find something similar in a thrift – I almost always do and of better quality.

Fashion is always about the comeback. I am so sick of seeing everyone wearing the same things. This is my way of getting out of it. That's why I started a blog about thrifting back in 2011. At the time, all the bloggers were displaying the same Zara dress. I wanted to show something different.

Does the sustainable aspect of thrifting appeal to you?
I think it's good, but I don't claim it's my primary motive. Yet I do want more people to get involved with using what already exists, so I have a project that upcycles existing clothes. The other day, I spotted this 'grandma dress', and my tailor transformed it into a trendy skirt. We have to stop producing so many clothes. The second-hand market is saturated. Did you know that some African countries aren't accepting second-hand clothes anymore? For me, it's a good thing. Western countries will be confronted by the massive amount of waste they're responsible for.

Now, tell us where you thrift!
Charity shops (Guerrisol, Emmaus), bric-à-brac stores – I especially like those out in the countryside; you find real gems for pennies – flea markets in Montreuil and Clignancourt and second-hand websites and apps.

How do you spot the hidden treasures?
I'm quite the fashion geek. Three years ago, when I moved in with my fiancé, I got rid of 22 years of fashion magazines. They're all in my head, so when I go into a shop I sometimes spot something and think, 'Hey, I saw that in a magazine in 1998!' Also, I look at people in the streets – their looks differ in every arrondissement. As I wander about, I'll notice, say, how a bourgeoise woman puts her clothes together in the seventh; the style traits of the so-called '*bobos*' [bohemian bourgeoisie] in the eleventh; and even you right now – I like your shirt and next time I'm in a shop, maybe I'll be thinking, 'Ah, this is what Aloïs wore last time I saw her.' If I see a garment that doesn't remind me of anything, I'll think of ways to combine it in my head.

Do you wear what's in your closet?
I have things I thrifted before my daughter was born [she is now 17]. That's why I don't buy items that are too flashy or eccentric. All my wardrobe is in rather bourgeois colours. I do put clothes aside. If they stay in my closet, I'll wear them again. Even if it's six months from now.

How do you mix all those clothes from different times of your life?
I mix and match to stay updated with

the current fashion. I can combine a jean jacket I have owned since the Eighties with a dress I got on Vinted and new earrings from a current collection, and the result will be super-modern. My aim is that when people see me they have no idea my outfits are almost 100 per cent second-hand.

What would you recommend to someone who's new to thrifting?
A young follower of mine asked me the same question. I told her the first thing to do was to get inspired – by Instagram, people in cafés…and magazines (they're not obsolete). Even if they have to make a living by working with the big brands, they're always the first to present what's coming next. My bible is *Vogue*.

'When I became a mother, I decided to give thrifting a try'

Jewellery

A few months ago, I was looking at my left hand when I noticed that the ring on my middle finger wasn't looking good. Bought three years before, it was made from gold-plated brass encrusted with five minuscule rhinestones. Two of the rhinestones had disappeared during the first year after purchase. I had them replaced at the shop. Now the other three had gone, too.

Meanwhile, on my little finger sat a gold ring with my initials engraved into it that my great-grandmother had given me when I was eight years old and it was – is – still flawless (and yes, it used to be on another finger in the past). The lesson was clear: this I-do-not-know-how-many-carat gold ring had been a true investment that has survived decades of doing the dishes (sigh!) and other risky encounters, while the gold-plated brass one had proved nothing but a waste of money.

So, I jettisoned it and decided henceforth to invest only in the real stuff that would be there for a lifetime and beyond. I went to an antique jewellery store on the Boulevard Saint-Germain and found a white- and yellow-gold 1930s ring. I had it resized. It's been on my middle finger for six months and I plan to spend the next 30 years with it.

Here are some guidelines on how to buy jewellery with eco-consciousness in mind:

'For forever' jewels

If, like me, you find changing jewellery every day a hassle, gradually build yourself a set of quality items that you'll wear every day. Consider brands that work with recycled gold or visit an antique shop, like I did for my 1930s ring.

'For fun' jewels

Avoid plastics and go for metals, non-synthetic resins and all things natural. There are plenty of cool pieces to be found second-hand and vintage.

Precious metals and stones

Gold, silver, diamonds and so on all have to be extracted from the earth, often causing great damage to both the environment and the workers who mine them (see the 2006 thriller *Blood Diamond*). For this reason, vintage jewels are a great option. There are also brands that manufacture jewellery from recycled precious metals and diamonds.

Pro tip

Pure metals can be infinitely recycled without loss in quality.

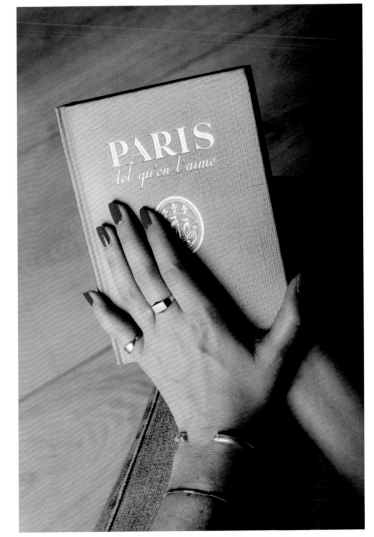

Timeless, classic pieces of jewellery are quite literally worth their weight in gold (or silver…)

Bags

When it comes to bags, I am the committed kind, having stuck with the same thick-leather black tote for ten years. It matches everything, doesn't scratch and can carry my laptop. I am married to it until death do us part. I asked Virginie from Atelier 2311, (*see* page 206), what you should look for when choosing the bag of your life:

Fabric

The thickest fabrics last the longest. Smoother textures are more fragile than others.

Tanning

Vegetable tanning is better for the environment but will be less protective of the leather. Chrome tanning offers optimal protection but creates more pollution (*see* page 172). However, new regulations covering this kind of tanning have made it next to harmless for nearby rivers and streams. If you scratch a chrome-tanned skin, the mark will remain almost invisible.

Handles and strap

Opt for a thick strap for durability.

Zips

Choose metal zips over nylon ones. They are studier, will last longer and don't use fossil fuels.

Ornaments

Unfortunately, nowadays almost every piece of bag jewellery is made of zamak, a zinc alloy. This oxidizes, and if two pieces are enmeshed, they sometimes corrode each other.

Is the brand relevant?

Branded bags can often be very hardwearing but this depends on the model. Some mid-range brands have excellent designs that survive the test of time.

Pro tip

You'll get more use out of a comfortable bag. If you like to carry your bag over your shoulder, make sure you can do so even when wearing a large coat, or that the bag has an additional, cross-body strap.

Glasses

When you want to say something is obvious in French, you say it's *'comme le nez au milieu de la figure'* – it's 'like the nose in the middle of your face'. That glasses should be chosen with great care is the embodiment of that saying. This applies to prescription glasses, as well as sunglasses, as both make an equally important statement.

Material

Acetate
Made of cellulose (*see* page 173), this is a favourite of glasses manufacturers and wearers alike – it's biodegradable, long-lasting and stylish. Some acetates can be charcoal-based, providing a surprising texture.

Titanium
Super-strong, lightweight and tough. Ideal for creating 'barely there' frames.

Steel
A good low-cost alternative to titanium.

Pro tips

• Combining different materials in a design can be both stylish and practical.
• Avoid plastic, which is prone to breaking and is non-biodegradable.
• When you smile, the bottom of the frame should never touch your cheeks.

Shape

Try on as many glasses as you can. Be daring with shapes and colours. There may be mishaps but also unexpected (pleasant) surprises. If you have only one pair, opt for a neutral model that will go with anything. There's nothing worse than being stuck with an eccentric pair that matches nothing (like those with coloured floral designs on the arms).

Colour

If you are pale with fair hair, try frames that are close to the colour of your skin, like soft pinks, transparent shades and light gold.

Blue-eyed girls can try silver or grey.

For others, try matching the frame with your hair colour. I suggest brunettes and redheads try browns, amber and tortoiseshell.

Dark-haired girls will look amazing in anything – lucky you.

Where to buy?

Try a trendy optician with a broad choice of frames including those by lesser-known designers.

Or try upcycled vintage frames. Plenty of brands have developed this concept over the last ten years.

If you find a vintage frame at a flea market that's a bit damaged, you could ask your optician to fix it for you.

Shoes

I am devastated when I'm targeted by ads (why, oh why?) marketing 'fabulous shoes at the price of a latte'. Such shoes CANNOT exist. Shoes are typically made of that noble material, leather (*see* page 172), and it takes a minimum of 120 steps to manufacture them. The fate of your cheap pair will be a quick death while your destiny will be arch pain and a not-so-fabulous look. Moreover, the production of said shoes will have hurt both the environment and the human beings who produced them.

If 'one of these days these boots are gonna walk all over' your ex, make sure they're a proper, well-made pair.

Material

The leather should feel like a 'live' fabric. Poor-quality leather shoes feel like cold, soulless plastic.

According to Jérôme Voisin, my cobbler (*see* page 213), vegetable tanning is a much better choice than chrome tanning as it lets the leather breathe and doesn't entail water pollution.

If you're vegan, stay away from plastic and choose a vegetable fabric like pineapple leather (Piñatex).

Overall feel

Shoes are made for walking so they should above all be fit for this purpose. Podiatrists recommend that you shouldn't be able to fold or scrunch up a shoe as this means your foot won't be properly supported. The heel counter should also be sufficiently rigid to support your foot.

Pointure Paris is a dream shop for all vintage shoe lovers

Insole

The insole should be a piece of leather that sits under the whole foot (sometimes, in closed shoes, the insole stops at the visible part to save money). This doesn't always apply to sandals, as the parts of the insole that will be visible when your foot is in the shoe need to match that of the straps (as shown in the picture, opposite).

A slight cushioning is a sign of comfort and good quality. It is especially important to have cushioning under the ball of the foot, particularly when you are wearing heels.

Outsole

Most of the time the outsole is made of rubber for better grip and waterproofing. Some shoes, often those made by luxury brands, have a leather sole. Even if this often means that the shoe is good quality, I recommend that you add a rubber sole after your purchase, otherwise water may soak in and ruin the whole shoe. You never know when a storm is coming, right? And I wouldn't want you to slip over either...

Stitches/glue

It's a sign of excellent quality when shoes have soles that have been sewn on. Aim for this if you buy flats or boots.

The best sewing technique for shoes is Goodyear stitching, which goes all around the outer upper part of the sole. As the stitches are located outside the shoe, they're hardwearing. Check that they are not losing microscopic fibres and are well coated. Blake stitching goes inside the shoe. You may notice the sewing on the insole.

Lots of delicate women's shoes are glued because this is the best technique to create a light construction. If this is the case, make sure there is no glue visible.

Pro tip

With regard to sneakers/trainers, eco and ethical early-birds like French brand Veja are an excellent choice.

The size

When it comes to feet, there is no such thing as 'one size fits all'. Always, ALWAYS, try shoes on before you buy them. Brands do not all use the same last: some come up narrow, some come up large, high, low, flat, bent…If you are buying online (for vintage for instance), the safest option is to aim for brands you already know and approve of. In the shop, try walking in them. They may feel a little stiff – remember, leather softens – but they should straightaway allow you to walk freely in a normal manner. If they don't, they're not for you.

The fit

There's a saying in French, *'trouver chaussure à son pied'*, which means 'to find your proper match'. The task of finding the right pair of shoes is very personal (ask Cinderella!). The most important thing is that the shoes are right for YOU.

The heel

'The thinner the heel, the faster it will become worn,' said my cobbler Jerôme when I asked him how to spot a good one. Block heels have a smaller risk of scuffing.

See page 212 for tips on how to care for your shoes

Chapter 5

Max Out the Lifespan

It's Time to Start Caring for Our Clothes

As a little girl, it mesmerized me to watch my dad cleaning his leather shoes. He took great care of the few pairs he had. Once a month or so, he would take them all off the shelf, clean them with an old sock and a used toothbrush (which I thought was a lot of fun), and finally polish them with a divine-smelling paste the colour of the shoe. I loved to see the dull brogues come back to life and would copy him using my own little shoe polishing kit.

I remember having my jeans mended by a seamstress when I ripped them, and the (many) stains on them being efficiently removed by my mother. Buttressed by this routine of mend and repair, our clothes hung around for many years…There's a toddler's denim romper suit in my family that did not only for me and my five sisters but also my baby niece. Thirty years later, the fabric has gone from dark to faded denim, but it still looks damn cool (and cute).

'Why have we stopped caring for our clothes?'

I feel that clothes are supposed to go through a long and fulfilling life, whether it's with you or their next owner. To achieve this, it's always a good idea to either buy quality in the first place or to buy second-hand.

In between, however, there's some maintenance to do – a routine job that too many of us have forgotten about. When I do closet editing for my clients, I often notice shoes whose soles should long have been replaced and sweaters that need de-pilling. I feel bad for the poor clothes. As valuable products, made by humans from natural resources, they deserve better care from their owner (that's you!).

Why have we suddenly stopped being careful about our clothes, letting them fall into such a state of disrepair that they are no longer wearable? Economic logic explains this odd behaviour. As the price of fashion dramatically dropped, it became a financial nonsense to have a garment repaired when the mender/craftsperson's charge would be almost as much as the original price… leading many people to toss aside the old and buy something new instead.

In 1960, the average French citizen allocated 14.1 per cent of their income to purchasing clothes. Thanks to lower prices and higher incomes, the 2015 citizen dedicated only 7.3 per cent of their income to clothing. As the cost of clothes as a proportion of a person's income has dwindled, the care given to those same clothes has decreased commensurately. The result? Seamstresses, cobblers and other craftspeople have one by one shut down their workshops. Nowadays, though, as we once again recognize that clothes should be non-disposable, people are going back to having their clothes repaired, leading to the development of a new generation of craftspeople.

In this chapter, I'll show you how to give your garments a long and happy life – whether under your own steam or with the help of a professional.

Wash Less

Thanks to Louis XIV (you know, because of the lack of toilets and bathing facilities at Versailles), the French people long ago acquired the reputation for being dirty. Little did we know that the early 21st century would acknowledge our (reputedly) minimalist washing habits as an 'eco-friendly gesture'. We were simply ahead of the times, that's all.

To be fair, the so-called developed world has pushed it a bit too far when it comes to being clean. Even washing-machine manufacturers have released a study which showed that 90 per cent of the clothes we wash aren't even dirty. Over-washing our clothes is damaging the environment in many ways. It consumes unnecessary water and energy and reduces our clothes' lifespan as each wash damages them at the microscopic level. What's more, synthetic clothes (*see* page 175) release microplastics into the ocean every time we wash them.

'Over-washing our clothes is damaging the environment'

How often should you wash your clothes?

When you feel they're not fresh anymore. Don't let some spurious rule dictate when you should wash a garment. Follow your instinct – listen to your inner cavewoman, who no doubt had an innate sense of when it was time to freshen up her mammoth-skin, single-shoulder dress.

When I was online searching for some scientifically validated guidelines, all I found was contradictory expert testimonies. So I conducted my own little enquiry, using an admittedly not very scientifically chosen panel garnered from Facebook and Instagram, to find out what led people to wash their clothes. 'Depends on how much I sweat in them' was the most popular answer. To me, this sounds like a reasonable criterion (because which of us really takes an accurate mental note of how many times we've worn something?).

The average recommendations my panel gave me were:
- tops: after 1–3 wears
- jeans: after 5 wears to twice a year
- other trousers: after 5–7 wears
- knitwear: after 7–10 wears (assuming you wear another layer underneath or sweat very little)
- jackets and coats: at the end of the season
- accessories such as beanies and scarves: 3 times a season (given what they absorb…).

In the case of a stain: IMMEDIATELY! Run to the washing machine, you fool (and refer to page 198).

Keep your wash basket fresh

Besides stains, the main reason your clothes get dirty (and smelly) is the development of bacteria, for which a warm and moist environment is the ideal breeding ground. As they settle down into the fibres, the bacteria quickly grow their oh-so-lovely families. Moist clothes can even cause mildew to develop. To avoid such a chain reaction, NEVER put wet clothes into your wash basket and avoid allowing clothes to linger there for months.

Give your clothes a breather

After a day's wear, your clothes deserve a break before being locked in a closet.

Instead of immediately hanging your coat on a crammed rack, hang it on a hook by itself so that air can circulate around it. Do the same with the clothes that you plan to wear the next day. You could put them on THAT chair in your room, as long as it isn't already drowning under layers of clothes. You could also hire a clothes valet – a piece of furniture designed to hang your clothes outside, not a domestic servant.

My aunt recommends hanging your knits out in the cold to freshen them up.

Pro tips

• Get a separate wash basket for your underwear and socks to avoid perfuming the whole basket with their musky smell. Compartmentalized wash baskets are also available.
• Regularly brush your coat to remove mud stains.

Wash Properly

My mother is a colour-sorting maniac when doing the washing. With six kids at home, she spent a good amount of her time hidden in the laundry room, feeding the washing machines (plural) with carefully sorted loads (for your information, my dad was doing the cooking). Now that I live by myself, and despite the fact that I have far fewer clothes to handle, I stick to her principles, provoking perplexed frowns from anyone who witnesses my 'folly'.

Here are my washing rules and tips, many of them inherited from my grandmother:

Pro tips

• If, like me, you're unsure about your ability to remove a stain, let your laundry specialist handle it.
• Be extra-careful the first three times you wash something new as the dye may run.
• Where should I put my Breton top? With the pale colours, *ma chérie*.

• Use a deodorant without aluminium salts to avoid yellow stains.
• Perfumes can stain delicate fabrics. Spray your skin rather than your clothes. If you appreciate them being lightly scented, spritz the area in front of you and walk forward into the cloud.

Remove stains before washing

Never put something with an untreated stain into the washing machine: it could become ingrained for good. Instead, treat the stains one hour before you put your clothes into the machine. You should rinse the stain after you have treated it and BEFORE you put it into the machine.

Treat different stains differently

As a general rule, rinse with COLD water as soon as possible. Sprinkling with baking soda and dabbing with white vinegar are generally valid techniques. Or take the item to a dry cleaner or laundry service.

Red wine

Immediately rinse the item in cold water (hot water will just cook the wine) using *savon de Marseille*. Do not rub the stain. Instead,

sandwich it between two pieces of cloth and press until the stain transfers onto them.

Fresh blood

Wash under cold water. Do not rub. Let it soak. You could try washing the stain with soap until it foams.

Dry blood

My *mamie* suggests gently scratching off any dried blood with a spoon before treating with a specially designed stain-removal product (while these may not be eco-friendly, sometimes using chemicals is preferable to losing ones clothes).

Berry juice

Soak the stain with lemon juice or white wine vinegar.

Grease

Sprinkle with powdered montmorillonite (this is a clay that is marketed in France as *terre de sommières*) and let it soak. It will make the stain disappear completely even before you wash it.

To restore whiteness

Mix baking soda and white vinegar together. When the mixture begins to fix, pour over the yellowish stains. If the yellowing is all over, replace your softener with baking soda during the wash.

Sort your clothes

According to colour

There's no need to be as pernickety as my mother; a rough-and-ready approach will do:
• whites and very pale colours
• pale colours
• deep colours.

According to fabric

Coarse fabrics such as jeans can damage finer ones. Avoid mixing them.

According to degree of dirtiness

While you should cold wash your knits, you'll probably need a hotter, more sanitizing temperature for your T-shirts and undies.

Use protection

• Put your more fragile garments (silk, cashmere, etc.) in a protective laundry bag so they don't rub against the drum.
• Use a specially designed Guppyfriend bag, to prevent plastic microfibres from reaching the ocean.
• Close any zips so they don't catch on other items.

Don't overload the drum

Your clothes can get scratched, and you may have to put the load on again if they come out not quite clean or wringing wet.

Go easy on detergent

Use organic washing powders in cardboard packaging. Otherwise, use a DIY recipe (I'm lazy about this, I confess). If you really

want to add a softener, use white wine vinegar instead of chemicals. Most importantly, whether it's an organic or chemical detergent, don't use more than the recommended dose – it can harm your clothes.

Choose the temperature wisely

The temperature on the label is the MAXIMUM the fabric can handle, not the recommended one. Washing at 30°C uses half the energy than washing at 60°C.

For wool, silk and fragile synthetics

Choose the cold wash/woollens or delicates programme.

For fabrics that aren't really dirty

20°C is enough.

For jeans

Use 30°C if you want to still be able to close the button afterwards.

For underwear

Use 40°C, handwash the delicates, or put

them in a protective laundry bag.

When you need to kill off stubborn bacteria

Use 60°C. Otherwise, wash at this temperature as little as possible.

Dry Properly

Now that you have been exposed to my mother's (and grandmother's) washing tips, make sure that you are giving just as much care and attention to the drying process.

Pro tips

• Allow whites to dry in the sunlight, which will help them stay white.
• Keep dark colours out of direct sunlight, or they'll lighten (think of them as vampires).

Where to dry your clothes

Optimally, outside with a fresh breeze. Otherwise, inside in the morning with open windows. Or just open the windows for a few minutes during the drying process. When the weather doesn't allow you to open windows, just wait for it to improve. If you can't wait…well, you'll just have to put up with it smelling less fresh.

How to dry your clothes

• Shake them out to keep ironing to a minimum (or to avoid it altogether).
• Hang tops upside down to avoid the shoulders stretching.

• Dry shirts on hangers.
• To preserve the shape of your knits, let them dry on a towel hung over a rail to let the air circulate from below. Don't hang them.

Avoid the dryer

The tumble dryer is the enemy of clothes and the environment. Use it as little as you can – doing so will also save you money. Woollens should NEVER be put in the dryer. Cotton and linen may also shrink significantly. In the winter, when you have to dry your clothes indoors – or in all seasons if you do not have an outdoor space – use the dryer's shorter programmes if you must.

Take big pieces to the dry cleaner

For coats, jackets and beaded evening dresses, the dry cleaner is the safest choice. Opt for a toxic- and chemical-free dry cleaner who uses as little plastic as possible.

The Art of (Not) Ironing

I hate ironing. My iron should be displayed in a museum of antiquities. I don't even own a proper ironing board. To avoid this abhorrent task, I have developed multiple strategies: getting my clothes to dry wrinkle-free, using a laundry service, and, recently, replacing my iron with a steamer. The good news is, avoiding ironing turns out to be very eco-conscious. Well, perhaps not the laundry service option.

What a poor patriot I am when you consider that the first thermostat iron was produced by a French company, Calor, in 1920. What's more, France issues laundry diplomas and awards to the most highly skilled workers in the field (they even get to wear a collar in the colours of *le Tricolore!*).

Wash and dry wrinkle-free

To keep wrinkling to a minimum, hang out your clothes as soon as your washing cycle is finished. Over-filling a washing machine (and/or a dryer) will leave extra wrinkles in your clothes.

Get a steamer

They typically use half the energy of a traditional iron. As it doesn't actually press the fabric, the steamer cannot deliver impeccable results, but lovers of imperfection and lazy people (like me) will be 100 per cent contented. Bonus: unlike the iron, a steamer cannot hurt your clothes.

Iron inside out

Use this technique for cashmere, velvet and silk. To avoid scratching, iron jeans inside out.

Use a press cloth for delicates

The French word for a press cloth – *pattemouille* (meaning 'wet paw') – sounds so quaint it might actually motivate you to iron this way. If you are in any doubt about your iron's lowest setting, or if your iron doesn't have a setting for delicate fabric like silk, place a damp cotton cloth over the item before you iron it.

Hire a professional

If you're really not in the mood to do any of the above, and can afford to do so, opt for a high-rated, eco-friendly dry cleaner.

Pro tip

Own an iron and a steamer? Use the iron for cottons and heavy-duty clothes, and the steamer for delicates (and lazy days).

Take Care of Your Wardrobe

Now that your closet isn't a mess anymore, what about keeping it clean, too?

Keep it fresh and dry

- Once a week leave the closet doors open when you're at work.
- The clothes in your wardrobe should always be perfectly dry and clean.
- Place a few lavender sachets inside (you'll feel like you're living in Provence). I also like to put in scented soaps.
- To absorb moisture, place a piece of coal inside a small box into which you have pierced some holes.

Give it a thorough clean twice a year

- Remove all your clothes.
- Clean the shelves. and other surfaces
- Put the clothes back.

If your closet still smells bad because the odour has got into your clothes, you could wash all of them. That's a lot of work, but you'll start back from a good base.

Keep out the moths

- Install moth-repellent cedar-wood blocks in your drawers.
- For your hanging clothes, there are special cedar-wood moth hangers.
- Once in a while, rub the blocks with sandpaper like a magic lamp to restore their efficiency.

Pro tip

Instead of cedar-wood blocks, my friend Lucie recommends using heavily scented cade juniper wood from Provence.

Pimp Your Bling

While you were trying out some of the storage methods I recommended in Chapter 1, you may have noticed that some of your lovely pieces of jewellery have lost their lustre. What about restoring them to their former, resplendent glory?

Treat it well

• Silver hates being taken to the swimming pool, where the chlorine will tarnish it.
• Perfume stains and tarnishes pearls.
• Gold-plate fears life in general and doing the dishes in particular. This leaves you with three options: buy pure gold instead (expensive but rewarding); go on strike as far as doing the dishes is concerned (dreamy); or remove your gold-plated rings each time you wash your hands (though you'll forget to do this half of the time and forget to put the rings back on the other half).

Clean them at home

Gold

Let your gold pieces soak in water into which you have put a teaspoon of baking soda before gently brushing with an old toothbrush (make sure the bristles are soft). Immediately dry completely.

Silver and other oxidation-prone metals

Line a small container with aluminium foil. Put the item of jewellery in. Add a coffee spoon of baking soda and some boiling water. Wait a few minutes. Dry with a soft, smooth cloth.

For difficult tasks, ask the jeweller

Sometimes the grimier parts of a piece of jewellery are impossible to clean without professional gear. Take them to a jeweller, who will be able to use an ultrasonic bath to clean them. He or she can also polish away scratches.

Give your jewellery a makeover

If you own jewellery featuring precious or semi-precious materials and you've got bored of them, you could offer them a second life by getting a jeweller to reshape them. Bored of that heavy, clumpy ring? You could have it transformed into several smaller ones. Loving the semi-precious stones on that tiara but have zero use for such a headpiece? Why not have them set into a necklace?

Alter It

While sorting your closet, you probably noticed a number of clothes that weren't the proper size. Whether they never were or whether your body has changed, what about having them altered so that they fit (that is, if you still like them)?

Make clothes smaller

It's easy for a skilled tailor/seamstress to take in a skirt or pair of trousers at the waist and butt. The waist can also be cinched on blazers and dresses. Your trousers and jeans can be even be altered to fit around the legs.

Make clothes bigger

Most good-quality trousers, skirts and dresses carry extra fabric on the inseam that can be used to make the garment go up one size.

Make clothes shorter

Jeans
Don't forget to stitch the hem with a yarn the same colour as the stitches elsewhere. You can also cut the bottom of jeans over the ankle bone with scissors for a cool frayed style.

Tailored trousers, skirts and dresses
Have them cut and the stitch reproduced.

Blazers and shirts
The bottom hem and the arms can be shortened. Pay attention to the positioning of buttons and pockets so that the alteration does not ruin the style of the garment.

How to find a good tailor/seamstress

Ask a well-dressed friend. Otherwise, ask the fancy clothes shop in town where it has its clients' clothes altered. Avoid any business that bills itself as a 'dry cleaning and alteration shop'. Tailoring should be a professionals-only job (though if it's just a question of shortening a pair of trousers, you should be fine).

Pro tips

• Dyeing will only work on natural fibres.
• The invisible stitching on the bottom of trousers and skirts often comes undone. Have a seamstress fix it.
• Altering shoulders is next to impossible. Make sure these are the right fit before you buy a garment.
• Don't let clothes you're going to have altered linger for ever in your entry-way. Schedule a day to take them to the tailor's.

Repair It

Treat those items that you still really want to keep, but that have become a little worn over time, with some overdue TLC.

Knits

Pills
Eloïse (*see* page 107) advises that you carefully shave your knits with a razor whose blades are not too sharp. For cashmere sweaters, invest in a cashmere comb.

Holes
If a hole isn't larger than the tip of your finger, you can sew it back together: find a yarn the colour of the knit and fill the hole both vertically and horizontally. Watch a tutorial online or have it done by a skilled seamstress/tailor.

Pulled yarn
This can be fixed but isn't an easy task. Ask a skilled seamstress/tailor.

Holes...

In jeans
These can be fixed by adding patches. Any alteration shop will do that. It's even better to go to a denim specialist who will fix the canvas itself.

In shirt elbows
You could add patches, or, more radically, have the sleeves removed.

Under the arms
Why not transform the shirt into a sleeveless one?

Broken zips
You can have the whole zip, or just the pull-tab, replaced.

Improve or change the colour
Sometimes the patina of age and wear adds character to a garment; sometimes it just makes clothes look dull. To give a washed-out garment a fresh start, consider dyeing it. There are plenty of ecological options available in the shops. If you're keen on craft, you could even make some homemade vegetable dyes.

Virginie Boukobza

Leather craftsperson and co-owner of Atelier 2311

What services does your enterprise provide?
We repair and renovate leather goods. We make an appointment with the client, see what they would like to change and then make it come true. We can even change the colour!

You founded the enterprise with your twin brother, so does this run in the family?
Ever since my brothers and I were kids, my mum always involved us in handicrafts and developed our creative side.

How did you train?
I studied furniture design and then, as I had a passion for fashion and liked leather, trained in leather craftsmanship before working for a leather goods company. My initial goal was to work in a small company where I could multitask. I didn't want to be stuck with a big manufacturer where I would repeat the same task all day long. That's how I discovered the activity of bag repair and renovation. It's a very little-known area that even many insiders haven't heard of. The company I was working with had started this part of the business just two years before I joined. It was super-interesting as we were working with so many different designs – each project was different.

Why do you think the demand for bag repair and renovation is growing?
I think people grow attached to their bags. Sometimes it's because they were a gift or a family heirloom. Many have a financial value, but a 'worthless' bag is very meaningful to the owner; they consider they have the perfect design so they stick with it.

What attracted you to this kind of work?
I love the idea that the bag already had a life. That we 'make it flat' [Virginie means this quite literally as she will often unsew the whole bag] before putting it back together again. Even after we have fixed and renovated it, the bag won't be new – the past will remain part of the way it looks, and for me this makes it even more beautiful.

Do you have heirlooms in your wardrobe?
I don't like throwing something away when I have memories attached to it. My mum likes to keep her clothes, even ones from when she was my age. My aunt, who used to be a stylist, does the same. It's great because they donate me amazing clothes that I wouldn't find anywhere else. Even my grandma's wardrobe contains some gems. Then I mix them with new clothes I've bought.

Are your choices influenced by a concern for the environment?

I've always valued objects and avoided chucking things away. This has increased since starting the atelier. We try every means to repair an item. We've no idea where our trash goes when we throw it away…

How do you deal with a damaged item in your wardrobe?

Well, I'm quite handy so I would often fix it myself. If it's a bit more tricky, I'll ask my mum, who is a talented seamstress.

How would you describe your style?

I like my clothes to be very different from each other so I feel I have a different look every day. I will mix classic items with something strong, and can wear a flowy dress one day and a boyish look the next.

Where do you shop?

I value quality over quantity. For small fashionable pieces, I still go to Zara, even though I'm trying to quit as I become more and more aware of the impact. Otherwise, I try to choose French brands that manufacture in France as much as possible. For shoes, I sometimes shop second-hand. I know how to make them look as good as new.

How many bags do you own?

Only three. My fave is a tiny vintage Lancel I found at a bric-à-brac fair years ago. It's so worn out but so perfect I can't let it go and I keep fixing it. My everyday bag is a leather tote I made for myself. It can carry everything I need. I also own a grey Miu Miu I got for my 18th birthday. I like the patina it has acquired over the years.

Do you wear all the garments you own?

Whenever I buy a piece of clothing, I ask myself first of all whether there's quality there, whether it will last, and whether it can be combined with several pieces I already own. I don't buy for the thrill, so they last.

How do you keep your clothes in good shape?

I'm very cautious with everything I own. I probably qualify as an obsessive! As soon as the rubber sole on a shoe gets worn, I have it replaced. I remove the bobbles from my sweaters with a razor blade. You have to be meticulous. I don't jam my sweaters next to one another in the closet, I use large hangers for my jackets in order not to damage the shoulder pads and I stuff my shoes with a shaper or paper and keep them in the box.

Cherish Your Leather Bag

Bag are probably our most mistreated accessory. We overfill them, we put them on the ground, we carry them around day after day…After all that hard graft they deserve some pampering once in a while. I asked leather craftswoman Virginie (*see* page 206) how to keep a bag in good shape:

Hydrate

Leather is an organic material. Like your own skin, you should hydrate it each month with a moisturizer (one specifically created for leather, *see* page 212). If you don't, the leather will dry out and crack, a deterioration that cannot be reversed.

Protect

Spray your bag once a month with a waterproof spray to prevent it from getting soaked and stained.

Store

Ideally, your bags should be stored standing, without being crushed against their peers. If you are a bit obsessive, like Virginie, the optimum is to stuff the bag with tissue paper or similar so it keeps its shape. She even keeps bags in their dust bag. The storage space should be dry and protected from sun and heat.

What can be fixed?

Pretty much everything – zips, handles, straps, piping, rips, holes, stains, colour…

Pro tips

- To enhance the longevity of a bag, when Virginie replaces handles she makes them thicker, and when replacing plastic piping she uses leather instead, since the plastic always ends up piercing the leather covering it.
- Shake your bag out once in a while to remove the dust and other particles inside.

Gisele

Social media manager

Coat

I found it in a thrift so long ago that I don't remember which. It was quite oversize for my frame, but I loved the very thick fabric and the design of the buttons so I bought it anyway. Plus, when you look inside, there's no label, so I guess it was handmade. At that time, my best friend's dad was a tailor so I asked him to cut off the sleeves. I wanted to give the coat a second life. He stared at me with eyes wide, but my best friend told him to trust my instinct and do what I asked. Not only did he cut the sleeves but he also narrowed the waist and fixed the fur collar and pockets. He really did an amazing job.

Sweater

As I have a long neck, I like tops that are high-necked. I found this chimney-collared one at Guerrisol. I paid 2 euros for it. I loved the cable knit and lavender colour. And it's my size, which is rare when you are petite.

Jeans

I found them at Kilo Shop. As I am really petite, it's difficult to find ones that are fitted at the waist without getting this 'diaper' effect. These do the trick. I roll them up a bit to show some ankle, and pair with heeled boots to elevate the style.

Boots

I got them new from a shop that sells only discounted samples next to where I live. They were a steal: premium-quality, 100 per cent leather for 50 euros. They have that mountain style but they're chic and the platform makes them super-wearable.

Necklace

My mum bought it in the Seventies with her first pay when she was about 18. Like every little girl, I was going through her stuff and must have chosen this one because of its floral design. It became part of my things… but I only started wearing it years later when I became more aware of fashion.

Ring

I always wear my grandmother's engagement ring. It's from the Twenties. It's quite peculiar with its gold-and-silver blend. I had to have it enlarged as my grandma had the tiniest fingers. It's also quite damaged. Once, I visited a man who specialized in fixing old jewellery. I said, 'It's very flawed, it's missing a stone…' to which he replied, 'So how would you look if you were a hundred?' He put it back into great shape.

Love Your Leather Shoes

I am so sad when I look through my clients' closets and discover very worn pairs of shoes, crying out for some care and attention. Sometimes, to soothe their pain, all it takes is a trip to their very own doctor, aka the cobbler.

In France, over the last 20 years, the number of cobblers – who have existed as a guild since medieval times – has halved. The drop in the price of shoes in tandem with the rise of fast fashion has led many people to decide that mending shoes just isn't worth it. Luckily, the trend is reversing, as people, conscious that our throw-away society is simply not sustainable, are increasingly getting their shoes repaired.

Meanwhile, shops are opening to welcome these new customers, like Atelier Constance run by my Montmartre cobbler, Jérôme (*pictured opposite*). He left his job in the music industry five years ago to open a repair shoe shop, just like his father before him. When I brought in my beloved heels for him to fix, I took the opportunity to ply him with questions while he was busy polishing shoes. With good maintenance, he says, quality shoes can easily last 20 years.

How can you keep shoes in good condition?

Rotation is key

What damages shoes most is not external but internal factors: the worst source of humidity comes from *within* the shoes (i.e. your sweat). A pair of shoes won't last if you wear them every day because the interior won't have time to dry out. To avoid this, wear your shoes on rotation.

Dust is the enemy

Dust hides in the 'walking folds'. To fight the invader, brush your shoes on a regular basis (with a shoe brush obviously). If you allow the dust to get into the skin, it will cause the leather to crack. For a thorough cleaning, you can use a special cleansing milk that's available in specialist shoe stores.

Proper storage

Flats should be stored using wooden lasts or shoetrees. Otherwise, your shoes will take on a banana shape as the leather dries and shrinks. For heels, you should use cushioned shoe shapers.

Nourish with products

Leather is stabilized skin so you need to take care of it. Invest in treatments developed by professional brands (preferably chemical-free ones). Cream is better than wax, as it lets the leather breathe and has a more natural-looking finish. It can even fix little scuffs. Apply it with a chamois cloth or horsehair brush.

Suede shoes need special care

Having removed the dust, use a hard brush to clean the dirty parts (for instance, where it's blackened around the heel). Don't use it all

When should you take your shoes to the cobbler?

Immediately

As soon as you buy a pair of shoes, have your cobbler add a rubber sole to the existing leather one. If you forget to do this, the leather sole will absorb humidity from the pavement, which will end up destroying your whole shoe.

Before the rubber heel and sole become worn

As soon as the soles show visible signs of wear, take them to your cobbler. If you don't, the damage will eat into the heel, eventually to the point where it is impossible to fix.

How to find a good cobbler

• They should exclusively do this job and not get distracted by other activities.
• Ask a trusted friend.
• Read expert recommendations.
• Search for internet reviews as these may be a good indicator of whether or not they are a skilled cobbler.

over, however. When they are brand new, spray a thin layer of waterproof product on them and repeat every 15 days if you're wearing them on a regular basis.

What can a shoemaker fix?

From the look of Jérôme's Instagram feed, the answer is ANYTHING. So why not take even your most damaged shoes to a trusted cobbler and see if they can salvage them?

Your Sneakers Deserve Love, Too

I'm kind to all kinds of shoes (except the ugly ones). My dear cobbler Jérôme is only trained in leather, so for professional help you'll need to go elsewhere: rejoice, as 'sneaker cobblers' now exist to save your dirty sneakers. In France, the first on the market was Sneakers & Chill. Check out its amazing work. However, there's also stuff you can do at home.

The body

Leather

Use a regular brush, water and soap (*savon de Marseille* is perfect). Gently scrub the shoe using the soap until foam appears, rinse the brush and reapply soap until the shoe is clean. Remove the foam with a towel.

Mesh

Carry out the same process outlined above. Don't wear them out in the rain and waterproof them on a regular basis.

Suede

Clean in the same way as regular suede shoes (*see* page 212). Again, don't wear them out in the rain and waterproof them on a regular basis.

The laces

Put them in a laundry bag in the washing machine and put them through a cool wash.

The sole

Vigorously brush with soap and water.

The smell

Never ever wear your sneakers without socks (use those low socks so you can pretend you aren't wearing any). If they already smell bad, let them breathe outside for a while and, if needed, use a shoe deodorant.

The shape

As with regular shoes, use shoe shapers to avoid your sneakers getting the dreaded banana shape.

Pro tip

Rotation is key with sneakers, too (*see* page 212). Otherwise the humidity can get trapped inside...and none of us likes that locker-room fragrance.

Consider Upcycling: It's Trendy

When I met Anaïs Dautais Warmel (*pictured right*) at a Fashion Revolution party a few years ago, I was struck by her vibrant style at a time when 'eco-fashion' mostly meant 'boring'. Since then her 'upcycling' fashion label Les Récupérables, which creates clothes from already-existing fabrics, has received a lot of attention. Here, I ask her about upcycling and on page 216 she shares some tips for you to try at home.

What is upcycling?

Upcycling is about taking a fabric that isn't used anymore to transform it into something of a superior quality. While recycling is about destroying a fabric to create another, upcycling upscales it.

Where do you find the fabrics you upcycle?

We use both post-consumer-use fabrics, such as household textiles that have been donated and collected, and pre-consumer-use fabrics from fashion houses who have small quantities of dead stock that did not meet their requirements – perhaps because they have a little flaw like a stain or something. Because we work on a small scale we can work around these and make the best out of the rest of the fabric.

Have attitudes toward upcycled clothes evolved?

Definitely. At first it was a bit foreign and odd to everyone. But now all these documentaries and press articles about the harms caused by fast fashion have made people aware of the benefits of buying clothes that were produced in a less harmful manner. Some people will giggle at the idea of dressing up in curtains like a modern-day Scarlett O'Hara, but I enjoy it.

A Lesson in DIY Upcycling

Anaïs's (*see* page 215) passion for upcycling began years prior to the launch of her brand. Craving to be different from others on a very limited budget, she was on a thrift-only dressing regimen long before it got trendy. Now, upcycling and customization services are booming. Why not get inspired and try doing some of them yourself before enlisting the help of a professional?

Try some of Anaïs Scissorhands' tips and tricks

- Cut the bottom of your jeans to shorten them and give them a raw edge (as pictured below left).
- Cut the bottom of your oversize jean jackets to shorten them.
- Cut your tops and sweatshirts to make them cropped.
- Play it like Frankenstein and swap the sleeves from a jean jacket for those from a sweater. (If you're a newbie, you might want to ask your trusted tailor/seamstress to do this.)

Small changes that make a big impact

Paint
- Use fabric paints and stencils to add stars (or whatever) to denims or any garments with smooth surfaces.
- Dye your clothes another colour.
- Create a tie-dye effect.

Embellish
- Replace boring buttons with ornamental ones.
- Apply a canvas on the back of a jacket.
- Roll a scarf around the strap of your bag (like Mathilde does, see page 102).
- Change the classic buckle of your belt for a statement one.
- Replace your bag's strap with a fancier one (you could even use an old necklace).

Enjoying my jeans customized by stylist Martine Anjorand (see page 128)

With more experience (or the help of an experienced tailor/seamstress), you can perform advanced transformations of your thrift finds. On social media, upcycling/sewing chains are booming. Glamorous 20-something Clara Victorya, for example, is encouraging thousands of young followers to learn sewing. Like Clara, try to see the potential of thrifts, clothes you inherited or clothes you used to love.

Some customization ideas you could try

- Turn a dress into an skirt + top ensemble.
- Turn an Amish-looking dress into a sexy one by cinching, shortening and cutting a low décolletage.
- Turn a leather trench into a jacket + skirt fringed ensemble.
- Turn an oversize jacket into a belted one by transforming the lower hem into a belt.
- Sew two silk ties together to create a geisha belt.

…The list could go on and on!

Watch videos and learn to see the potential of thrifted clothes for yourself before briefing your tailor/seamstress (or learning how to sew). I personally won't go anywhere near a needle, but if you're a 'crafty person' this could become a great new hobby for you.

Hire an artist to customize your items

In an era where a fast-fashion dress can be found anywhere on the planet (oceans included), we all crave differentiation. Responding to market demand, lots of brands and shops are now offering customization services as a way of attracting customers. More interestingly, a new generation of artists are offering customization services for ready-to-wear pieces. Bags, shoes, T-shirts, shirts, jeans and so on can be painted or embroidered by specialized artists. It's a bit like tattoos for your clothes. Lots of those talented craftspeople can be found on Instagram.

Make New Outfits From Your Old Clothes

In Chapter 1, we left none of your clothes without a pairing thanks to the 'style-proofing lesson' (*see* page 38). Now that you've come this far, couldn't you extend the lifespan of your own clothes even more by rekindling the appeal they once had for you? Reignite that old flame, as they say.

Here are a few easy 'style recipes' that EVERYONE can try. (Call me the Mlle Ratatouille of fashion.) And for more recipes, refer to my first book, *Dress Like a Parisian*. Put it next to your wardrobe and start styling!

Rethink your approach to colours and prints

Top an all-white outfit with a coloured or printed layer
A green jacket, a beige trench, a checked coat…

Wear an all-black outfit in different fabrics
A timeless knit, chic black pants, patent leather shoes, leather belt with a big buckle…

Combine pale colours together
White jeans + pastel shirt + mother-of-pearl jewellery + beige trench + camel shoes.

Add a pop of colour to a neutral outfit
Classic white T-shirt + jeans + beige trench + an ultraviolet beanie you can spot miles away.

Dare a makeup detail the opposite colour to your top
• Lilac sweater with bright coral lips.
• Green scarf with fuchsia lips.

Combine prints of the same shades
• Brown checks with orange flowers (*see* Nawal in her suit with orange bag, page 67).
• Black background prints together (*see* Amel in her dress and bomber, page 141).

Mix different prints
Flowers, stripes and plaid love each other, I swear (the proof is Lena – *see* page 63).

Accessorize

Dress basic and add as many items of jewellery that you can find
This works with something very casual – a T-shirt with layers of bling – or very refined, such as a black silk shirt with layers of bling.

Belt your jeans
And while you're at it, why not try a fun buckle? This can transform an outfit. If your outfit is already complicated, go for a basic belt.

Belt your jackets
And give them a whole new style (*see right*).

Add fabulous shoes
Dress basic and finish with a pair of patent red leather Mary Janes (or anything that you can spot from a distance).

Try funky tights
Always works with plain dresses.

Change the way you wear it

Tuck in oversize clothes and roll up the sleeves
A slouchy sweater can go from teddy bear to sexy when you tuck the front into your skinny jeans or tight skirt and add a belt. This works with oversize shirts, T-shirts…

Button up thin cardigans
Instead of wearing them open over your dresses, close them over your naked skin and tuck them into your jeans and skirts like Nineties Kate Moss.

Layer, layer, layer!
Be experimental, especially in mid-season:
• white T-shirt + jean jacket + trench
• white T-shirt + hoodie + blazer
• white shirt + jumper + coat

…and so on!

Index

accessories 142, 219
  storage 50–1
  style-proofing 38
addictions 16, 35, 37
Adöm 89
age
  and heritage 63
  older women 126
alpaca 164, 165
alterations 71, 124,
  204, 208
Ananna, Amel 124,
  126, 141, 148,
  149–51, 218
Angora 164, 165
animal welfare 165, 167
Anjorand, Martine 128,
  129
army gear 114
Atelier Constance 212
auctions 110–11, 116

bags 40, 51, 64, 65,
  102, 103, 181
  choosing 186
  heirlooms 70, 71
  leather 113, 128,
    129, 186, 209
  repair and
    renovation 207
  vegan alternatives
    172, 188
Bangladesh, Rana
  Plaza garment
  factory 119, 162
basics 26–7, 40, 41
  colours 26, 40
  cost per wear 156
  embellishments on 26
  pairing 20, 21, 38
  repeated items 35
  shopping for 138–9
  statement pieces with
    30, 39, 140–1
  style-proofing 38–9
  unwanted 19
Beaugé, Marc 66

belts 40, 51, 98, 99,
  139, 168, 169, 216,
  218
  leather 113
  statement belts 116
Birkin, Jane 8
blazers 40, 204
blouses 46, 115
Bonnefoy, Nawal 60, 67,
  69, 82, 118, 119–21
boots 32, 33, 40, 64, 65,
  98, 99, 102, 103, 168,
  169, 210, 211
  high leather 113
  shopping for 138
Boukobza, Virginie 206,
  207–8, 209
bourgeois heritage 62–3
bracelets 40, 49, 90, 98
branded items 94–5,
  150, 153
  bags 186
  counterfeits 96
  donating 42
  eco-conscious 69
Breakfast at Tiffany's 28
brooches 70
buttonholes 176, 177
buttons 176, 216

Canada 34
cardigans 219
caring for clothes
  194–205
cashmere 164–5, 199,
  201, 205
catwalks 68
Céline 68
cellulose acetate 173
Chanel, Gabrielle
  ('Coco') 59, 66, 153
Chardonnet, Count
  Hilaire de 173
charity shops 42, 43, 73,
  84, 92, 93, 182
Chaussettes Orphelines
  174

chokers 32, 33
Chu, Nadia 32–4, 33
city heritage 62
Clauzet, Mathilde 61,
  74, 75–7
climate 41
clothes swapping 80
coats 26, 40, 46, 128,
  129, 210
  caring for 196, 197,
    200
colours 19, 40, 218
  basics 26, 40
  repeated items 35
Comptoir des
  Cotonniers 62
compulsive personality
  16, 37
consignment stores 42,
  82–3, 84, 100, 101,
  142
cost per wear (CPW)
  156–7, 158
costume parties 142
cotton 166
country, heritage from
  62
CPW (cost per wear)
  156–7, 158
curvy women 124
customizing items 217

Damas, Jeanne 8
decluttering 14–25
  the crushes 17, 20–1
  the dependables 17,
    22–3
  the 'evil twins' 35
  lifestyle changes 36
  six-month rule 24
  style personality types
    16, 37
  the unwanted 17,
    18–19
  where to donate 42
denim 112, 171
  see also jeans

dependable clothes 17,
  22–3
donated clothes, recycled
  174
donating 42, 43, 73, 142
dreamer personalities
  16, 37
Dress Like a Parisian 8–9,
  218
dresses 28, 29, 41, 128,
  129
  altering 124
  silk 168, 169
  storage 46
drying clothes 200
dyeing 204, 205, 216

earrings 28, 38, 40, 49
eccentric clothes 21, 24,
  140
Econyl 174
embellishments 26, 115,
  216–17
espadrilles 9, 28, 29

fabrics 164–75
  recycled 174
  synthetic 175
  upcycling 215–17
  wood-based 173
family influences 62–3,
  181
  heirlooms 70–1, 207
Farouil, Lena 28, 29
fast fashion 7, 11, 68,
  119, 132
  cost per wear 157
  donations 42
  outdated 18
  and quality 162–3
Faye, Martine 127
Firth, Livia 142
flaws in clothes 22
flea markets 96–7, 97
folded clothes 46, 47
Fontanel, Sophie 126
former-life clothes 21

friends 62, 80–1
Friere, Élodie 102, *103*

garage sales 96–7
Germany 11
gifts, unwanted 80–1
Gisele *31*, 210, *211*
glasses 28, *29*, 50, 187
gloves 50
Goldsmith, Claire 28
Gossip Girl 119
The Great Gatsby 66
grooming style 34
Guinut, Olga 90, *91*

H&M stores 9, 132
hanging clothes 46
hats 40
heels 38, 45, 212
heirlooms 70–81, 207
hemp 171
Hepburn, Audrey 28
hoarding patterns 16
holes in clothes 205
Hopaal 174

immigrant heritage 63
impossible matches 23
influencers 60, 69, 126,
 135
Instagram 60, 69, 75,
 76, 84, 109, 121, 162,
 217
ironing 201
Italy 11

jackets 32, *33*, 84, 102,
 219
 army 114
 basics 26
 caring for 196, 200
 denim 112
 leather 113
 oversize 122
 storage 46
jeans *27*, 32, *33*, 40,
 112, 151, 210

altering 204
caring for 196, 199,
 201
high-waisted 9
raw-edge 9
repairing 205
second-hand 98, *99*
shopping for 139
storing 47
style-proofing 38
upcycling 216
and weight
 fluctuations 36
jersey fabric 166, 170
jewellery 32, 40, 98,
 116, 184–5
 for bags 186
 basic 26
 caring for 203
 'for forever' jewels
 184
 'for fun' jewels 184
 heirlooms 70, 71, 72,
 90
 storage 48–9
 style-proofing 38
jewellery boxes 49
jumpsuits 114

Kardashian, Kim 82
knits 166
 basic 26
 oversize 122
 repairing 205
 storing 46, 47
 washing 196
Kondo, Marie 47, 50

lace 166
Lan Anh 63
Laubez, Eloïse 100, *106*,
 107–9, 205
layering 219
leather 113, 172
 bags 113, 128, *129*,
 186, 209
 caring for 209,

212–13
 shoes 188, 212–13
Ledet, Manon 64–5
Les Récupérables 215
lifestyle changes 36
linen 170
linings 178
loafers 38
Louise Paris *101*
lyocell 173

McCartney, Stella 11
Mad Men 66
makeup 34, 52–3,
 119–20, 218
Mazaré, Alice 98, *99*
medals 72
men's clothing 78–9
Merino wool 164
minimalism 76–7
Miu Miu 68
modal 173
mohair 164
moths 202
Mozemba, Francine
 60, 126, *180*, 181–3
Mugler, Thierry 32
multiple purchases 16

necklaces 40, 49, 210,
 211
nettle 171
nostalgia 20, 60, *61*
nostalgic personalities
 16, 37
nowhere to wear
 clothes 20
nylon 175

occasion wear 142, 157
online shopping 125,
 155
 buying vintage 84,
 94–5, 116
 influencers 60, 69,
 126, 135
 selling online 42,

149–50
organic cotton 166
organic silk 167
outdated clothes 18, 20,
 140
oversize clothes 122,
 124, 219

pairing clothes, basics
 20, 21, 38
Paris 6, 96, 120, 132
personal shoppers 145
petite figures 124
Pinterest 60, 66
plaid patterns 9
Pointure Paris *189*
polyester 175
practical personality
 type 16, 37
practical use/style use
 rule 136
practicality 141
prices 11, 153, 156–8
Prigent, Judith 168–9
prints 178, 218
pullovers 26

recycled diamonds 185
recycled fabrics 174
renting occasion wear
 142
repairs 205, 208
Repreve 174
rings 32, 38, 40, 49, 72,
 90, 98, 184, 210

salespeople 146–7
sandals 38, 40, *81*, 115
scarves 40
 heirlooms 70
 men's 78
 silk 70, 115
seams 176
seasonal storage 44, 45
second-hand clothes 11,
 82–92
 myths about 82–3

perks of buying 83
shopping for 86–111
sewing 176
sheep's wool 164, 165
shirts 90, *91*
altering 204
basic 26
men's 78, *79*
oversize 122
repairing 205
style-proofing 38
white *27*
shoe racks 45
shoe trees 45
shoes 32, *33*, 40, 64, *65*,
90, *117*, 128, *129*, 219
flats 40, 45, 115, 212
heels 38, 45, 212
material 188
sandals 38, 40, *81*,
115
shopping for 88–91,
139
sneakers 45, 190, 214
storage 45, 212
style-proofing 38
vegan alternatives
172, 188
vintage 105
see also boots
shopping
adopting the purchase
143
for basics 138–9
buy less dress better
132–3
buying only the best
144–5
changing rooms
146–7
cost of clothes 195
eco-conscious 158–9
examining before
buying 176–8
mistakes 134–5, 151,
153
occasion wear 142

practical use/style
use rule 136
and time 159
wearability 152
see also online shopping
silk 167, 173, 199, 201
sisters 80–1
six-month rule 24
size 122–4, *125*, 152
altering to fit 204
shoes 191
skirts 40, 90, *91*
altering 204
hanging 46
leather 113
pleated 115
shopping for 139
Slimane, Heidi 60
Sneakers & Chill 214
socks 50, 128, *129*, 174,
214
split personalities 21
stains 196, 198–9
statement pieces 26, 30,
31, 39, 40
belts 116
cost per wear 157
steamers 201
stitches 176
storage 44–51
accessories 50–1
folded clothes 46, 47
hanging clothes 46
jewellery 48–9
makeup 52–3
seasonal 44, 45
shoes 45, 212
Stranger Things 66
style use/practical use
rule 136
style-proofing 38–9, 40,
218
suede shoes 212–13, 214
sustainability 162–3,
182
hemp 171
linen 170

wood-based fabrics
173
sweaters 40, 99, 102,
210
heirlooms 72
shopping for 139
storing 47
style-proofing 38
synthetic fibres 175

T-shirts 32, *33*, 40, 116
basic 26
cost per wear 157
heirlooms 72
oversize 122
shopping for 139
storage 47
style-proofing 38
tall women 124
thrift stores 82, 84,
86–7, 92, 120
curated 88, *89*, 120
ties 79
tights 11, 50, 175, 219
tops
altering 124
oversize 122
washing 196
trench coats 26, 40, 64,
65, 102, *103*, 114
trends 9–11, 140, 153
outdated 18
trousers 40, 46, 115
altering 124
hanging 46
heritage 64, *65*
leather 113
shopping for 139
washing 196
The True Cost
(documentary) 162

unwanted clothes 17,
18–19, *19*
unwanted gifts 80–1
unworn clothes 24
the crushes 17, 20–1

upcycling 215–17
utility jumpsuits 114

vegan alternatives to
leather 172, 188
Veja 190
Victorya, Clara 60, 217
vintage stores, high-end
104, *105*, 116
Vipiana, Céline 60
viscose 173
Voisin, Jérôme 188, 191,
212, 213, *213*, 214

wardrobe care 202
Warmel, Anaïs Dautais
215, 216
washing clothes 108,
196–9
watches 28, *29*
weddings 142
weight fluctuations 36
weight gain 20
Westwood, Vivienne 11
wood-based fabrics 173
wool 164–5, 199
workwear 114
worn-out clothes 18, 21,
22, 42

YKK 178
YouTube 60, 69

Zara 132, 182, 208
zips 178, 186, 205

References

Introduction
page 9 'podcast asking random people about the latest trends': Aloïs Guinut, 'Qui fait les tendances?', *Programme B*, podcast, Binge Audio, 2019.

Chapter 1: Wear Your Closet
page 17 'a la Marie Kondo': see, for example, Marie Kondo, *The Life-Changing Magic of Tidying: A simple, effective way to banish clutter forever* (Vermilion, 2014).

Chapter 2: Heritage
page 66 'The more educated you get about fashion, the less you buy': Marc Beaugé, 'Entreprendre dans la mode', podcast #120, soundcloud.com

Chapter 4: Quality is Queen
page 167 'An 1840 article in *The Times*': *The Times*, London, article CS117993292, 12 October 1840.

Chapter 5: Max Out the Lifespan
page 195 'In 1960, the average French citizen allocated 14.1 per cent of their income to purchasing clothes…': https://www.insee.fr/fr/statistiques/2550287

All websites accessed March 2020

Contributors

Adöm, rue de la roquette – pictured on page 89 @adomroquette

Albayrac Kenan, rue vivienne – pictured on page 205

Alice Mazaré – interviewed on page 98; pictured on pages 98, 99, 123 and 163 @alice.mazare

Amel Ananna – interviewed on page 149; pictured on pages 141 and 148 @envoituresimoneparis

Anaïs Bouitcha – pictured on pages 112 and 117

Anaïs Dautais Warmel – interviewed and pictured on page 215 @lesrecuperables

Élodie Fiers – interviewed on page 102; pictured on page 103 @rougeprofond

Eloïse Laubez – interviewed on page 107; pictured on page 106; Louise Paris store pictured on page 101 @louiseparis.fr www.louiseparis.fr

Francine Monzemba – interviewed on page 181; pictured on pages 71 and 180 @frannfyne

Gisele – interviewed on page 210; pictured on pages 31, 210 and 211 @giseleisnerdy

Irma Notorahardjo – pictured on pages 85, 154 and 179 @irmanoto

Jérôme Voisin – pictured on page 213 @atelierconstancemontmartre

Judith Prigent – interviewed on page 168; pictured on pages 105, 114 and 169 @moujikparis

Lena Farouil – interviewed on page 28; pictured on pages 29 and 63 @lenafarl

Manon Ledet – interviewed on page 64; pictured on pages 65 and 83 @madeinfaro

Martine Anjorand – interviewed on page 128; pictured on page 129.

Martine Faye – pictured on page 127

Mathilde Clauzet – interviewed on page 74; pictured on pages 61 and 74 @mathildeclauzet

Nadia Chu – interviewed on page 32; pictured on page 33

Nawal Bonnefoy – interviewed on page 118; pictured on pages 118 and 67 @nawalbonnefoy

Olga Guinut – interviewed on page 90; pictured on pages 81 and 91

Onayza Sayah – pictured on pages 27, 58 and 138 @onayzasayah

Pointure Paris – pictured on page 189 @pointureparis

Virginie Boukobza – interviewed on page 207; pictured on pages 206 and 209 @latelier2311

Acknowledgements

Merci to Alison Starling for inviting me to publish my first book and this, my second. To Juliette Norsworthy, Polly Poulter and all the publishing team for guiding me through both projects. To Jessica Durrant for illustrating this one.

To Irma Northorandjo for her beautiful photographs and precious support…and to her baby Alix, who came on the ride with us from the inside.

To Eloïse Laubez, Amel of En Voiture Simone, Francine Monzemba, Nawal Bonnefoy, Virginie of Atelier 2311, Mathilde Clauzet, Lena Farouil, Manon from Made in Faro, Judith Prigent from Moujik, Nadia Chu, Martine Anjorand, my sister Olga, Alice Mazaré, Élodie aka rougeprofond, Giseleisnerdy, Rebecca from Adöm, Onayza Sayah, Anaïs Bouitcha, Martine Faye, Elysées Couture and Iris Noble for posing and sharing.

To the experts who gave me their invaluable insights: Virginie Ducatillon from Adapta, Jérôme Voisin from Atelier Constance, Andrée-Anne Lemieux, teacher at the Institut français de la mode, and Anaïs Dautais-Warmel from Les Récupérables.

To my family: my sister Zoé, Lucie Rousseau, *mamie* Brigitte, my parents and Isabelle.

To my online unpaid translation support team: Agathe Marian, Angela Linneman, Anne-Laure Roty, Caroline Dartailh (especially for her 'butter-less croissant' suggestion), Tom Lagatta, Phil Bloomfield, Antoine Escuras, Matthew Benney and Josh Hug.

To all my friends, clients and followers who shared their thoughts with me.